The Borderlands of Education

The Borderlands of Education

Latinas in Engineering

Michelle Madsen Camacho and Susan M. Lord

LEXINGTON BOOKS
Lanham • Boulder • New York • Toronto • Plymouth, UK

Published by Lexington Books
A wholly owned subsidiary of The Rowman & Littlefield Publishing Group, Inc.
4501 Forbes Boulevard, Suite 200, Lanham, Maryland 20706
www.rowman.com

10 Thornbury Road, Plymouth PL6 7PP, United Kingdom

British Library Cataloguing in Publication Information Available

Library of Congress Cataloging-in-Publication Data

Camacho, Michelle Madsen, 1969–
The borderlands of education : Latinas in engineering / Michelle Madsen Camacho and Susan M.
Lord.
pages cm
Includes bibliographical references and index.
ISBN 978-0-7391-7558-3 (cloth : alk. paper)—ISBN 978-0-7391-7559-0 (electronic) 1. Women
engineers—Education—United States. 2. Hispanic American women—Education (Higher)—United
States. 3. Sex discrimination against women—United States. 4. Sex discrimination in higher educa-
tion—United States. I. Lord, Susan M., 1965– II. Title.
TA157.5.C36 2013
331.4'820008968073—dc23
2013005428

♾™   The paper used in this publication meets the minimum requirements of American
National Standard for Information Sciences Permanence of Paper for Printed Library
Materials, ANSI/NISO Z39.48-1992.

Printed in the United States of America

Contents

Acknowledgments

This work was supported in part by a collaborative grant from the National Science Foundation (NSF) Gender in Science and Engineering Research (GSE-RES) program (0734085 & 0734062). The opinions expressed in this work are those of the authors and do not necessarily reflect the views of the National Science Foundation.

The original artwork used on the cover is titled *Woman Rising*, by Tamara Adams. Michelle was moved by this image when she saw and purchased it a few years ago at the Portland open market. Later, she gave it to her McNair mentee, Daina Sanchez, a first-generation Zapotec American student, as she embarked on her graduate career following in Michelle's footsteps in the PhD program at the University of California, Irvine (with instructions to pass it on to her first PhD student). We are grateful to the artist for letting us use her inspirational piece.

We would like to thank Dr. Jolene K. Jesse, our NSF program officer, for her support and encouragement of our work. We are also indebted to our research group for their contributions to our larger project, including Dr. Matthew W. Ohland and Russell A. Long of Purdue University, Dr. Catherine Brawner of Research Triangle Educational Consultants, Dr. Richard Layton of Rose-Hulman Institute of Technology, and the late Dr. Mara Wasburn of Purdue University. We are grateful to our excellent External Evaluation Panel (EEP) for this GSE program including Dr. Sue Rosser of San Francisco State University, Dr. Bevlee Watford of Virginia Tech, Dr. Barbara Olds of Colorado School of Mines and now NSF, Dr. Catherine (Kitty) Didion of the National Academy of Engineering, and Dr. Rebecca Brent of Education Designs, Inc. We wish to thank Donna Llewellyn and Sharron Frillman for assistance with our focus groups.

This book would truly not have been possible without the tremendous support of our families. Michelle thanks her mom, Nancy Beatriz, *por tu amor y cariño* and for being there with the grandchildren so that this project could be completed. Susan thanks her parents, Rose Marie and Arthur Lord, for their lifelong support and enthusiasm for her work and this book. We particularly owe a debt of gratitude to our husbands, Robert (Bob) Walter and Victor Wei-chung Chang, for all of their love, their helpful discussions that have improved the book, and for keeping things going at home while we worked on this. Thanks to our children for their patience, love, and understanding of the importance of this work: Daniella, Savanna, and Nathaniel Walter and Marissa Rose Wen-lan Chang and Kyrielle Wen-su Lord. Special thanks to Marissa Rose and Kyrielle for graciously helping with checking references. Our lives are richer because of all of you.

Acronyms

ABET   formerly the Accreditation Board for Engineering and Technology

ASEE   American Society for Engineering Education

EYH   Expanding Your Horizons

FIE   Frontiers in Education (Conference)

HSI   Hispanic-Serving Institution

HHE   High Hispanic Enrollment (Institution)

IEEE   Institute of Electrical and Electronics Engineers

NSF   National Science Foundation

SHPE   Society of Hispanic Professional Engineers

STEM   Science, Technology, Engineering, and Mathematics

STS   Science, Technology Studies

SWE   Society of Women Engineers

Chapter One

The Borderlands of Education

The polished marketing materials used by college admissions offices to re-cruit students to undergraduate engineering programs often deliberately fea-ture women. This imagery belies the reality that engineering is one of the last bastions of exclusionary education and one of the few remaining sex-segre-gated disciplines in academia. Though Title VII of the Civil Rights Act enacted major social and cultural shifts by barring discrimination on the basis of race and sex in 1964, and Title IX mandated educational equality on the basis of sex in 1972, half a century later it is incredible that 82% of engineer-ing bachelor's degree recipients in the United States are men. While many people think these issues have been addressed and are no longer problematic, and despite gender parity in many academic majors, there has not been dra-matic progress in engineering. And while there is considerable variation among academic institutions and between engineering subdisciplines, the national data in Table 1.1 glaringly demonstrate that engineering education remains both highly gendered and racialized.

Our interdisciplinary and multi-methodological book considers issues of race and gender broadly and focuses on Latinas in engineering specifically. Quantitative data provide summaries of information at a glance—in Table 1.1 for example, we see that Latinas are only 2% of all engineering students earning bachelor's degrees. Qualitative data, by contrast, offer us in-depth information about meanings, motivations, and the experiences of students through their own eyes, such as how Latina women might feel in a classroom of almost all men. While 2% of Latinas may seem like a small group, we propose that studying this population teaches us much about the culture and climate of engineering itself. We juxtapose quantitative data about retention rates in engineering against focus group narratives by Latinas who are navi-gating some barriers and succeeding in the process. What began as an explo-

1

Table 1.1.   Number and percentage of U.S. citizen and permanent resident bachelor's degree recipients in engineering.

Race/ethnicity	Gender	Number of bachelor's degrees in engineering	Percentage (%)
White	Male	38,320	60.9%
White	Female	7,327	11.6%
Asian/Pacific Islander	Male	6,480	10.3%
Hispanic/Latino	Male	4,316	6.9%
Black	Male	2,238	3.6%
Asian/Pacific Islander	Female	1,786	2.8%
Hispanic/Latino	Female	1,261	2.0%
Black	Female	858	1.4%
American Indian/Alaska Native	Female	75	0.1%
American Indian/Alaska Native	Male	272	0.4%
Total Women		11,307	18.0%
Total Men		51,626	82.0%
Grand Total		62,933	100%

Source: National Science Foundation, National Center for Science and Engineering Statistics, special tabulations of U.S. Department of Education, National Center for Education Statistics, Integrated Postsecondary Education Data System, Completions Survey, 2009.

ration into the high persistence rates among Latinas in engineering (revealed in our earlier research) evolved into this project: a broader critical assessment of the field of engineering education itself.

While the quantitative data in Table 1.1 depict the contemporary numerical landscape in engineering education, they do not provide a picture of how a Latina member of the 2% may perceive her engineering classroom. Foreshadowing the qualitative data of our research subjects (in Chapter 4), below we offer a narrative contrasting two students, Catalina and Joe, written from the perspective of Catalina, a first-year Latina engineering major. This narrative emerges from our research and participant observations in engineering education. It is also informed by our experiences of what it means to be a minority in many classrooms.

CATALINA'S STORY

"What about biology? There are lots of women doctors." Catalina remembered what her high school guidance counselor had suggested for a possible major. Standing in the doorway to her first engineering class in college, looking at a roomful of engineering majors, Catalina quickly drew her breath in. Not one familiar face. Catalina looked at the room number again. Engineering Hall 228. Intro to Engineering was a required course for all first-year engineering students. This was the right place. She smiled, stiffening her posture, and walked into the classroom of 30 students. She noticed that she was one of only a handful of women in the class, and the only Latina, but she wasn't surprised since this was what she had been told engineering would be like.

Looking at the men in the class, she sensed they were more comfortable than she felt. She could tell by the way they stretched their legs out across two desks, hollered "hey, what's up" at each other from across the room, or stood in clusters talking animatedly about a high school robotics championship. One student, Joe, seemed to recognize her from an earlier class. "Hey," he nodded to her. Catalina smiled and said "hi" even though she did not recognize him. The classroom was crowded so she walked to an empty seat in the front corner of the room. Joe seemed to have many friends including a roommate in this class. Catalina's roommates, by contrast, were studying biology and psychology, so they did not share any of the same classes this semester. Joe was talking about a fraternity keg party and mentioned it to the guy sitting behind Catalina, whom he seemed to know from his high school. None of Catalina's high school friends were majoring in engineering, and she knew that only some were going to college.

Five minutes before class start time, the professor arrived and began adjusting the projector. He finally looked around and introduced himself. As he gave an overview of the class topics, Catalina wondered whether she would team up with anyone for the study groups that the professor was mentioning. She sighed but knew deep down that it would work out. "That's just how it is," she thought to herself and began writing notes.

While struggling to decipher the professor's handwriting, she thought back to her favorite teacher from high school, Mrs. Sanchez, from AP Calculus. Mrs. Sanchez, who wrote her a letter of recommendation, had faith in her and always encouraged her choice of engineering given her strong math and science grades. Although Catalina was a straight-A student in high school, she knew that some people thought the only reason she was here was because of affirmative action, and that annoyed her. She was also tired of being repeatedly questioned about whether she really wanted to be an engineer. Even her mom asked her why she wanted to be an engineer and what she'd do if she didn't like it in her first year. She was thinking about joining

SWE, the Society of Women Engineers, and SHPE, the Society of Hispanic Professional Engineers, since she heard that could help you get a good job. Mostly, she did not think too much about whether she belonged or not. She just planned to work hard and graduate.

ENGINEERING AS AN EXCLUSIONARY SPACE: THOUGHTS ON RACE AND GENDER

Recruitment, not retention, in engineering education is the primary problem that explains the low numbers of women and minorities. Catalina and Joe are equally likely to graduate with a bachelor's degree in engineering (see Chapter 3 for data on engineering retention rates by race/ethnicity). Nevertheless, Joe, a White man, does not even consider how his race and gender configure the social equation. Being both male and White in engineering, Joe is among the majority. He may not notice that the rest of the group is predominantly White; it is the social norm in engineering. Whiteness in the United States is the default backdrop against which other racializations are constructed— White is not seen as "ethnic" (even though an analysis of ethnicity among Whites would yield great differentiation). Rather, among non-Hispanic Whites, Whiteness is read as nonracialized, as nonethnic, as the norm. A single White person in a group of all Blacks or Latinos would likely immediately notice his or her own differences, and perhaps become hyperaware of his or her own subjectivity. But among a majority group of other Whites, he likely will not notice or reflect on his own racialization. In the context of the engineering classroom, for those occupying the dominant majority, there is no impetus to pause and reflect on one's own identity or racialized awareness, other than to notice those around who look different. For Whites, the dominant script constructs Whiteness as "invisible"; those who do not pass as White are the minority "Other." White students will sometimes erroneously say, "I have no race or ethnicity."

While not unique to engineering, the cognitive marking and categorizing of social bodies fits with the historic racialization of people in the United States. Since its founding, the United States has relied on laws and policies to help us understand where "outsiders" fit into our social hierarchy. Waves of immigrants around the world are greeted with mixed feelings by host countries, creating national discourses of who belongs and who does not. These national debates are played out and reinforced by everyday practices, such as where we live and which neighborhoods we visit, our cultural tastes including what and where we eat, and who our closest friends are. For example, if as a child you grew up in a neighborhood where bars were on all the windows of the homes, throughout your youth this would be the norm; but if you did not grow up in this context, then you might learn to call this type of neighborhood "bad" or "the ghetto." Operating here are two social forces: (a) how people are associated with, and identify with, their neighborhoods and (b) a legacy of residential housing codes and racial covenants that created segregation (by preventing certain groups from accessing loans to buy in White neighborhoods). Whether "bars on the windows" is constructed as normal or deviant depends on one's social location and context.

Both our individual conceptualizations of what is normal and what is deviant are also influenced by larger structural forces. Structural forces include social institutions that create or perpetuate the status quo, such as systems of education, policing and the law, housing, and development. Social forces, such as how media stereotypically portray people of color, perpetuate differences and continue to construct race and class stratification as meaningful, despite the popular ideal that we should be a "color-blind" society. We are not a color-blind society because individual and institutional racism continue to haunt, and shape, our society. While the wounds of racism affect us all, they are lived and remembered on a daily basis by people of color.

In engineering, similarly, gender differences are perceived most acutely by women. When people talk about gender, many commonly think of it as a woman's issue, not a man's (even though both bear gender). A paucity of research exists on how masculinity is constructed in engineering, or what it means that engineering is a masculine space. Women adapt in engineering by making their gender less apparent, by trying to fit in, by minimizing their differences. These are strategies women in many positions of corporate leadership have adopted in order to be taken seriously; volumes of books are written for women who want to tap in to the "old boys' network." While women have achieved near-gender-parity in the ranks of medical and law schools, the statistics reflecting the gender gap in engineering education and industry continue to look surprisingly lopsided. Despite these numbers, the structural sexism in engineering remains largely invisible. There is a persistent cultural taboo to talk about these issues outside of sexual harassment workshops or conference presentations devoted to topics of gender. Thus, the gendered component of engineering is relegated to one that women should grapple with, rather than a problem with which all engineers should be concerned.

As Table 1.1 shows, being a White male in engineering is statistically normative. A critical analysis reveals this normativity is a position that offers advantages and embodies privilege. Contrasting Joe and Catalina in the opening narrative, we see that when one occupies a privileged position, it is not always perceptible.

PRIVILEGE IN ENGINEERING

Sociologist Michael Kimmel uses the metaphor of wind to describe the subtlety of privilege (2010). If you are walking into the wind, the force of the wind holds you back, it makes you walk more slowly, you squint your eyes; it can be chilly. In short, you are aware of the wind and progress feels slow. By contrast, if the wind is constantly at your back, you hardly notice it. It puts a lift in your step, you walk seemingly effortlessly, you reach your destinations more quickly. There is no force holding you back.

In engineering, to be White and male is to have the wind at your back; you do not have to think much about the natural forces that sustain you and allow you to feel comfortable with relative ease. You can make mistakes without people attributing it to your race or gender. You can ask questions or draw attention to yourself without worrying if people will make judgments about you based on race or gender. You can easily find many others who look similar to you. Your speech and accent, the jokes you tell, the food you eat, and your social habits seem normal. People do not question your academic abilities on a regular basis, or wonder if you are an "affirmative action" token. You move along fluidly; your race and gender seem invisible to you.

When the large majority of those in leadership positions are from a relatively homogenous group, it is often those who are in marginal positions that work to convince the majority that the mechanisms of marginalization are real. This is the case in engineering education. Because the United States is built on ideologies of individualism and meritocracy, most people commonly think about racism as, simply, prejudice or individual discrimination. Racism is equated with "mean behavior" and not seen as a structural force that produces and perpetuates inequality at a systematic level. The absence of women in engineering is explained away as a problem having to do with lack of interest rather than examined in terms of how engineering education repels women.

Engineering students and faculty are both the stakeholders and agents of change. If the problems are largely invisible, however, there is no impetus for change. The status quo of engineering feels uncomfortable to those who fail to see themselves represented; for them, engineering is a lonely place and allies need to be sought out with effort. By contrast, for the majority of engineers who see themselves represented effortlessly, who never have to think about finding allies that share similarities, the status quo is an invisible luxury. Sexism and racism are not visible problems to them or of much concern on a daily basis. The environment, the formal and informal social organization of engineers, the transfer of knowledge, and a set of shared values all support the status quo. Although it is less common today to ask why social organizations are needed to support Black engineers or women engineers, occasionally someone will say, "Why isn't there a society for White engineers?" without realizing that almost all of the societies are in fact societies of predominantly White engineers.

THE CULTURES OF ENGINEERING

Engineering is not a monolith. Engineering includes many disciplines, and diverse definitions circulate of what it means to be an engineer or to do engineering. Among engineers, tacit knowledge exists about the social ordering of engineering subdisciplines. Typically engineering involves some element of design, grounded in scientific and mathematical theories, to create products, systems, or processes to meet specified needs. Engineers share a culture characterized by common sets of meaning of rigor, implicit and explicit messages about the value of a "hard" curriculum, and established patterns of work ethics grounded in modes of problem-solving capabilities. How are these meanings generated, maintained, and transmitted? While reflexivity about engineering in the broader social context blooms in a few engineering education departments, among feminists, sociologists, and historians of science and technology studies, there is still a huge amount of terrain to explore about how the history of engineering contributes to contemporary internal modes of exclusion.

Talking about contemporary racism can be an uncomfortable subject for engineers, leading to feelings of guilt, denial, annoyance, or anger. Why might this be the case? Why aren't more engineers champions of conversations engaging questions and leading efforts in antiracism? Why does this seem like such a radical question? When 82% of all engineering majors are men, 72.5% are White, and 61% are White men, what is seen by the majority is all that is seen. The issues of institutional racism are not salient, meaningful, or addressed habitually because they do not affect the majority; rather, they are seen as minority issues that should be championed by minorities. In fact, this is how antiracist work has always been in the United States from the times before desegregation to beyond Title IX. The corollary of racism, White privilege, is a largely unrecognized concept in engineering with only recent explorations (Eschenbach, Lord, Camacho, & Cashman, 2012). For some, the term *White privilege* itself may even seem divisive. Right-wing antiacademics call it a politicized term used to empower underrepresented minorities at the expense of those who have embodied the American ideal of meritocracy and worked hard individually to make gains. A social justice perspective, by contrast, would suggest that racism stems from action and inaction; those with privilege have a duty to become allies to combat racism and structural inequalities.

The status quo that engineering is a White male space has only been challenged by significant numbers of Asian American undergraduate students and international graduate students. The discourse about these changes, however, echoes in the media with xenophobic ideas about how international competition with India and China will take away American jobs or how Asian Americans are taking away opportunities from more deserving White students. In U.S. engineering circles, leaders recently have begun to talk about "changing the conversation" and diversifying engineering by bringing new people to the table. But there have since been few mainstream conversations about how engineering itself as a discipline might benefit from systematic changes. According to Donna Riley, an engineering professor at Smith College and author of *Engineering and Social Justice*,

> Generally, engineering students learn to think *analytically* only in certain ways appropriate to technical analysis. For example, we learn to break problems down into small parts, solve the individual parts, and then work back up to a solution. We typically do not come away with the ability to think *critically*, to question what is given, or to question the validity of our assumptions, because we are too busy learning the essentials of problem solving. For this reason, we often cannot see the larger context of the problem we are working. We lose sight of the big picture, especially if we are sleep-deprived from too many hours in the lab and doing problem sets. We do not learn, with any depth, critical approaches from the humanities and social sciences, and we do not learn many communication skills beyond writing technical reports and giving PowerPoint presentations. Thus, it is no wonder that some engineers may come across as apolitical or clued out about contemporary issues outside of technology. (2008, p. 41)

Riley's conceptualization of "engineering mind-sets" suggests that the apolitical nature of engineering stems from an uncritical acceptance of authority and a narrow technical focus. In *Engineering and Social Justice*, Riley conducts a critical analysis of jokes about engineers to illustrate the nuanced "mind-sets" that characterize them. From a structural perspective, these jokes unveil the stereotypical characteristics of engineers. The themes that emerge in Riley's analysis include a willingness to help other people and solve their problems (even it if results in one's own demise); a tendency toward "brute force methods of problem solving" with a focus on precision and perfection; positivism and a blind trust in the scientific method; a lack of sociality compared with an excess focus on technicality; a militaristic mind-set (because of job orientation); uncompromising objectivity; and political inaction (2008, pp. 35–38). Riley suggests that these jokes beg reflection, interpretation, and analysis. From a social perspective, jokes seem funny when they resonate with common popular knowledge; they circulate as a means to poke fun about social groups. Engineering jokes may also reflect exaggerated characteristics that engineers hope to dismantle. Taken together, the jokes suggest an overly detailed, technical, and dispassionate view of the social world, to the exclusion of other worldviews. From a cultural perspective, studying these jokes and their meanings provides a window into how engineering communities perceive and critique themselves and their internal culture.

ENVISIONING CHANGE: ENGINEERING AND THE SOCIOLOGICAL IMAGINATION

Sociologist C. Wright Mills coined the phrase "the sociological imagination" to suggest that social outcomes are shaped by context and history, not merely by individual action. Mills asserts that social phenomena cannot be understood from a singular analytic perspective, and that "personal troubles" are linked with "public issues" (1959). He used the sociological imagination to understand the larger historical scene as it relates to choices individuals make. Applied to the paucity of women and underrepresented minorities in engineering, the sociological imagination would suggest that the dearth of these groups in engineering is not related to their individual, rational choices not to pursue careers in this field. Nor is it related to a lack of interest on their part in engineering. Rather, the sociological imagination would suggest that the context and history of engineering provide the lens through which to best understand their exclusion. In engineering, culture is not a monolith—diverse subgroups within engineering continue to make and contest meaning about the social contributions of engineers. These meanings, however, emerge from a long history in engineering; one that is entrenched in a militaristic background that continues to shape engineering applications. Looking retrospectively at the context and growth of engineering as a discipline, it is easy to see how its resistance to change has produced rigidity in the curriculum and narrow occupational outcomes. Systematic change in engineering can only occur with analysis and pointed interventions aimed at understanding the environment that supports engineering; the social organization of engineering; the transmission of knowledge in engineering; and the system of values, messages, and meanings that engineering produces. What are the forces of stability and varieties of tradition that produce stasis, and how can these be disrupted or managed to produce new visions of social justice in engineering?

Mills urges social researchers to examine the interplay between micro and macro perspectives. In engineering, how do women, for example, talk about their microexperiences? How do their experiences fit within the macrocontext? The late Gloria Anzaldúa, renowned Chicana author and cultural theorist, uses the metaphor of the "borderland" to describe how outliers fit within the landscape of the norm. She theorizes exclusion using the Spanish term *mundo zurdo* to describe the spaces of contradiction, tension, and ambiguity in which these outliers reside (Anzaldúa, 2007). Applying her framework to women of color in engineering, for example, would suggest that these women occupy the social margins of engineering, embodying "difference" and signifying a social "other." The result is a confining space for women of color in engineering, where allegiances are fractured. Anzaldúa's framework suggests that the exclusionary nature of engineering produces rigid categories and places women in a liminal status, perpetually in a crossroad of wanting to belong but never really fitting in. In these interactional borderlands, "subjects may feel like outsiders to exclusive social arenas" (Segura & Zavella, 2008, p. 539).

The borderlands in engineering, however, also represent a fruitful terrain of possibilities and potential. Structural forces create a particular exclusionary social context, but within this context social changes germinate. For women and underrepresented minorities in engineering, this increasingly means raising awareness and developing counternarratives to slowly transform the culture of engineering from within, and bringing new and diverse perspectives to enrich the field. For example, this includes adopting innovative pedagogies and reaching across communities for inspiration and innovation. The marginalization can inform the praxis, allowing us to shed new light on internal problems by asking critical questions.

IMPETUS FOR THIS BOOK: FULL DISCLOSURE

This book emerges squarely from the borderlands, with the hope that the voices from the margins will strengthen the center. We write this book from unique interdisciplinary vantage points, combining the expertise of both sociological and engineering perspectives. Within these academic traditions, we bring our unique perspectives as a Latina sociologist and a White woman engineer; we both have PhDs and are tenured full professors. In engineering, women professors typically represent between zero and less than 10% of the entire engineering faculty. Unlike engineering, sociology has equal numbers of men and women. However, only 3.9% of professors in the United States are of Latino descent (National Center for Education Statistics, 2003, Table 254). We share our personal narratives here because they represent an example of how synergistic networks align to produce a text such as this. Also, within social science research, it is common for researchers to disclose the conditions that affect their interpretations.

Though we both are faculty at the University of San Diego, we are in separate academic units and there are few opportunities for cross-disciplinary interactions. Serendipitously, we met at a campus function for women faculty. We quickly learned that we shared interests in community-service learning and liberative and feminist pedagogy. On a personal note, both of us are mothers of young children (a marginal position among most tenured professors), and we have had our share of marginalizing racist or sexist experiences in the ivory tower.

Depending on your background, you may think that this collaboration will result in a "biased" analysis of engineering education. A research methodologist, however, would argue that all accounts are biased; in fact, the misperception that objectivity exists is what reproduces inequality. In other words, whose voice is objective? The best we can do as scholars is to strive for objectivity using systematic data and analysis, and to be transparent about our biases.

Camacho's Account

I became interested in engineering education by special invitation; Susan Lord asked me to help her design a research project exploring how engineers practice engineering through pedagogy. With seed funds from the National Science Foundation (NSF), we set about conducting exporatory qualitative interviews and applying a quantitative method called Cultural Consensus Analysis among two groups of engineers. The first group of engineers consisted of anttendees of the Frontiers in Education (FIE) conference that is known for presenting innovations in engineering education. We used a sampling technique called "purposive sampling" to identify experts from among these attendees. We then interviewed them, and later coded and analyzed the data. We compared their narratives with those of engineering professors who had not attended such conferences or presented or published on pedagogy in engineering. We later presented our research findings (Lord & Camacho, 2007a, 2007b; Lord, Camacho, & Aneshansley, 2008). Following this exploratory foray into the field of engineering education, I was invited to participate in writing an NSF proposal with Susan Lord and Matthew Ohland of Purdue University examining a large, longitudinal data set based on my interest and expertise in social science research design and issues in gender/race/ethnicity. The project was successfully funded and numerous papers emerged from the research (Brawner, Camacho, Lord, Long, & Ohland, 2012; Camach & Lord, 2011a; Camacho, Lord, Brawner, & Ohland, 2010; Lord, Camacho, Layton, Long, Ohland, & Wasburn, 2009; Ohland, Brawner, Camacho, Layton, Long, Lord, & Wasburn, 2011).

As a first generation college graduate, I am often asked by my students and mentees about my personal story, that is, how and why I ended up in academia. My journey in academia toward the PhD was less of a pathway and more of a labyrinth. Born in St. Francis Hospital, I lived on the south side of Chicago until I was three. My mother, an immigrant from Bolivia, met my White Chicagoan father by chance on a train. Three years after I was born, they moved to Southern California. My father, a high school graduate, had trouble finding work, and the night job he held unloading boxes financially strained the marriage. My mother worked as a waitress for Howard Johnson's restaurant to try to make ends meet during this time. The two divorced. My Bolivian grandmother worked as a housekeeper for a well-off family not too far away. Eventually my Bolivian grandparents moved close by to help my mom raise us kids, and I grew up speaking Spanish fluently and understanding tidbits of the Quechua indigenous language that interspersed their Spanish. My mother, who had studied typing and shorthand, worked in a myriad of positions; she always knew that her life would be easier if she had furthered her education. She nagged me daily to keep up my grades so that my fate would be different.

Our home had bars on the windows, and the alley was spray-painted with the signs of the local gangs. Less than a block away was the local donut shop, where I worked when I was 15. The donut shop was also a local evening hangout for prostitutes and a pimp who would sometimes entertain me with his magic tricks when donut sales were slow. I didn't realize then that these early experiences would plant a seed for my research on the informal economy, the urban underclass, stratification, race, gender, and social inequalities that I would later specialize in as a PhD student.

In high school I held side jobs, at the donut shop but also intermittently at a variety of fast food restaurants. Because I spoke fluent Spanish, I could easily translate for the local customers. I tried to stay out of trouble for the most part, unlike two of my best friends who became pregnant. I enrolled in a community college course to take chemistry so that I'd be eligible to take physics in my senior year, and I elected to take a typing/shorthand class so that I'd be able to work at higher-paying summer jobs. Haphazardly thinking about college applications, I applied to three locally and was accepted to all.

My greatest source of joy and companionship was my grandmother, who moved in with us and served as the backbone of our household. From her, I learned to cook with love, to be patient and caring, to be spiritual, and to dance. Leaving for college was most painful because she was ill, and I was her primary caretaker. The first week of classes, I attended the Latino Welcome event, where I met the women who would be my best friends throughout college. I also met the directors of the Chicano and Latino Student Support Services, and they assigned me a peer mentor who guided me through my initial adaptation to the college environment. I joined MEChA (Movimiento Estudiantil Chicano de Aztlan), a group that promotes student empowerment through community activism, and I was elected to the Executive Board every year thereafter. The students in MEChA and administrators in the Student Support offices sustained and guided me. They taught me through our informal conversations and recommended readings so that I learned what none of my classes offered about ethnic identities, social inequalities, and institutional discrimination. We hosted Cesar Chavez, the labor movement organizer, for a special dinner event, and in those years I volunteered as an activist for the United Farm Workers' movement. I began to find my voice as a leader.

A popular White male professor consistently appreciated and encouraged my insights in classes and suggested that I consider graduate school. At the time, I was a communication major and was working as a paid intern at Univisa, the largest international Latin American media conglomerate. My hope to be a bilingual news reporter for a Spanish network was short-lived because every window office in our building was held by a man. The media business was highly gendered and I could easily perceive "the glass ceiling" that limited the mobility of the women. With clarity that this was the wrong field for me, I turned down their job offer.

Around the same time, a professor who had read several Spanish essays of mine suggested that I apply to PhD programs. Without a clear plan beyond an idea that higher education needed structural change and diversity, I wrote applications to top graduate schools theorizing the underrepresentation of ethnic minorities in higher education and proposing a plan to diversify academia through activism and by transforming the curriculum. Later that year, I earned my BA with high honors based on academic achievement, and two leadership awards, which were my proudest achievements. Though I had several offers for graduate school, I selected the one closest to home so I could be near my ill grandmother. I was awarded a Presidential Fellowship at the University of California in Irvine in an interdisciplinary program in Anthropology and Sociology. Today I am convinced I would not be an academic had it not been for the peer support and mentorship I received from other activists whom I continue to respect deeply, and from the two professors who saw potential in me and reached out.

I mention these circumstances because they illuminate the push and pull factors that affect my academic pathways. As social science scholars, we often study what we know or what is dear. My research interests in race, gender, social class differences, and inequalities are influenced by my own historical lens and my subjective understanding of what it is like to explore the borderlands of academia.

Lord's Account

I became an engineer because my father (also an engineer who was a physics professor) said I had to major in engineering because I was good at math and science, and he thought it would be a good career. He thought my experience would be like his. I was well prepared academically from high school but not really prepared for the sexism that I would encounter. I grew up believing that success in math and science had nothing to do with gender.

I knew no boys who were better at these subjects than I, and my parents strongly encouraged me. However, despite being a straight-A student, I did not apply to technical schools because I was afraid that I would fail at engineering and it did not make sense to me to major in something like English at a place like MIT. I was accepted at several schools. When I visited Princeton, one of the admissions counselors asked me why I wanted to be an engineer since it was mostly boys. I remember thinking this was very strange and not encouraging. By contrast, I visited Cornell at the invitation of the Society of Women Engineers (SWE). I was welcomed by the women students there and decided to enroll.

In college, I was initially shielded from much of the sexism because I was very active in SWE. When I was a junior, I felt completely unprepared when an engineering professor made a sexist remark when I asked him for help during his office hours. I asked him a question about a homework problem and he refused to answer and closed my book. Then I asked him a problem about the "double stub tuner" that we had been discussing in class earlier that day. He said something helpful and I thanked him. His response to me I remember verbatim: "That's OK. I understand. Girls have these kinds of problems. I have a wife. I have a daughter." Honestly, it took me a few seconds to comprehend what he had said because I was still thinking about the double stub tuner. I don't remember what happened next except that I left quickly. I do remember the horrible feeling that I had. All he could see at that moment was my gender. He didn't know anything else about me: my grades, my work ethic, my abilities. Even if I had tried to explain any of those to him (Cornell gave 4.3 for an A+ so my GPA was actually over a 4.0), I knew that it would have no impact. I was a girl and that's all that mattered.

This experience of feeling powerless ignited a strong desire to help other women. As vice president of SWE, I was in charge of programming. After this experience, I told everyone I knew in SWE about it and organized a speaker from Women's Studies to present results of a campus survey at one of our meetings. This was a radical thing for SWE. (Later I would learn that we were very much in the liberal feminism tradition: don't talk about sexism, focus on positive, etc.) We invited the dean of Engineering, who looked incredibly uncomfortable the entire time. He had a hard time accepting that there was sexism at Cornell or in engineering. As I have reflected on this experience, I feel fortunate that it was mild compared to what many others have had to endure. I am grateful that it opened my eyes and helped prepare me to seek out resources to help myself when I later confronted worse situations in graduate school.

When that professor made that comment to me, I was flabbergasted. I had heard stories of women being denied engineering degrees a long time ago and knew there had been discrimination. I really thought that it was gone and that even if people still thought that women were unsuited to engineering, they had the sense not to say it out loud, especially a professor!

I chose to go to graduate school because I wanted to teach. My parents are both teachers and one set of grandparents were teachers, so it is "in my blood." I was awarded two different fellowships for graduate school. One advantage of being a U.S. citizen majoring in engineering is that there is a lot of money to support this. Being a woman meant even more money was available. Both fellowships allowed me to choose which graduate program to attend. This was a tremendous benefit. The NSF fellowship was for three years and is considered quite prestigious. The Bell Labs Graduate Research Program for Women (GRPW) was only for women, to encourage more women to get PhDs in engineering. It was for the duration of the degree program, included a summer job, a mentor at Bell Labs, a trip once per year to visit your mentor at Bell Labs (my parents lived close to Bell Labs so this was essentially a trip home), and other benefits such as travel support for conferences, books, and a yearly reception on campus. I debated between these two fellowships for a long time. I was drawn to the NSF one since it had none of the affirmative action stain. Finally, I decided that this GRPW fellowship was one of the few advantages that I had encountered as a woman engineer and, frankly, it was a better deal. So I took the GRPW fellowship and am very grateful to Bell Labs.

Graduate school was very difficult but not in the ways I had expected. I knew that women were 10% of electrical engineering graduate programs but I had not realized that 10% would be one woman: me. I felt very isolated. I kept finding myself in the position of being asked to represent half the human race when my peers would ask me "What do women think?" So I decided to use one of my few electives to take a feminist studies class. I was astonished that people actually thought about the issues that were raised here, such as why women earned less than men or how gender roles are socialized. Men were about 10% of the classes in feminist studies, but everyone, students and professors, bent over backwards to make the men feel welcome. No one did this for me in my engineering classes. Being the only woman out of 25 students in my research group, it was hard to separate out meanness to Susan from discrimination against women. These classes helped to give me a larger perspective on problems of gender equity. They helped to shape my approach and language when I would talk with my male colleagues so that I was less defensive and personal. At the time, I never imagined how helpful these classes would become in my later research and even in writing this book.

The most difficult challenges for me in graduate school were not technical but social. There were many jokes, comments, and other seemingly small incidents (now I would label them as "microaggressions"). Then, I started to hear disturbing stories about bachelor parties and other group activities with

female strippers that my research group was "famous for." At first, I as-
sumed that my advisor had not participated or known about them. I was
appalled when I learned that he not only participated, but also paid for them.
The hardest thing that I had to do in graduate school (and perhaps my life)
was to confront my advisor about this issue. These happened prior to my
joining the group, and for over a year, I tried to close my eyes and hope they
would not happen again.

Then, when I was about to go to my first conference with the group, I felt
that I had to say something. I did not want to be put in the position of having
to go to such an activity. The feelings of exclusion and stress were weighing
heavily on me. I talked to many people, carefully crafted what to say, and
practiced so that I could get through it without becoming emotional. I had to
say something but realized that I was risking my career in electrical engi-
neering if he responded badly. I tried to put things in larger perspective,
thanked him for his support of me, recognized his desire to have more women
in the group, explained how these activities went beyond his personal life
since his attendance legitimized them as group activities, and tried to desexu-
alize the issue by emphasizing the exclusionary nature of the activities, say-
ing I would also feel excluded if he took the group to the men's sauna. I
focused on asking him not to do this anymore and was careful not to back
him into a corner or sound too angry. At the end, he said "I'm so glad you
felt like you could come talk to me. I guess I shouldn't do that anymore."

Then he basically did not speak to me for a year until on an accreditation
visit at another university, he met a woman graduate student who had to
change her research area because of sexism by her advisor. My advisor was
astonished. He came back and said to me, "I thought about when you came
to talk to me. I realized that you either must have been much braver than I
thought or much more stupid." At my PhD defense, he said that I had been
an important member of the group and had "hit him over the head with a few
well-placed 2x4s." Most people attending had no idea what he was talking
about, but my family and friends understood.

I have been angry about these experiences, but rather than dwelling on
them I have tried to use what I have learned to improve the situation. I was
willing to put up with this because I am determined and had a great support
system of family and friends. As an engineer, I am usually focused on the end
result—in this case, surviving my engineering education so I could become a
professor and be in a position to make a difference. However, I can under-
stand how others would be turned away. It is not just that women are "not
interested" in engineering. There are many other factors at play that need to
be examined and acted upon. These experiences have made me ask critical
questions and want to reach out to others in disciplines like sociology to help
answer these questions.

BORDERLANDS OF EDUCATION: OUR VISION

This book is aimed at researchers who study underrepresented groups in engineering and are interested in broadening participation and ameliorating problems of exclusion. We hope it will be useful to scholars in the fields of multicultural and higher education, sociology, and cultural anthropology, as well as cultural studies and feminist technology studies, and all researchers interested in the intersections of science, technology, engineering, and math (STEM), race, and gender. This resource will be useful for policy makers and leaders looking to address the culture and "chilly climate" within engineering.

As we write this book, we bring with us our authentic experiences as a woman in engineering and a Latina in the academy. Thus we each have insider and outsider perspectives on aspects of Latinas in engineering. Forging such linkages between people with diverse perspectives is critical to doing this work. Insiders have the advantage of in-depth knowledge but suffer from an inability to see beyond the culture in which they are immersed. Outsiders have the advantage of seeing the culture more distinctly but lack investment in the discipline so that they can too readily launch criticisms without considering the consequences. By reaching across disciplinary borders, we can illuminate the nuances and multiple exclusionary forces that shape the culture of engineering and the participation of Latinas. This is one type of intersectionality. Our work also uses an intersectional lens by considering both race and gender, something that is uncommon in research on underrepresented groups in engineering. Thus, this book represents the first focused treatment of Latinas in engineering, an endeavor that is long overdue.

One of the primary reasons that a book on the topic of Latinas in engineering has not been produced to date is because of the low numbers of women in the field of engineering, preventing systematic data analyses. Our large, multi-institution, longitudinal data set allows us to disaggregate by race and gender. We rely on primary and secondary sources and incorporate an integrated mixed-methods approach combining quantitative and qualitative data. Together, our analysis of the voices of Latina engineering majors, obtained by our focus group research, breaks new ground in the literature on STEM education and provides an exemplar for future research on subpopulations in these fields. Our research was sponsored by the NSF through a Gender in Science and Engineering (GSE) grant. This book builds on work published in the *Journal of Hispanic Higher Education* and *Latino Studies* (Camacho & Lord, 2011b; 2013).

We write and theorize from the literal socio-geographic space that *is* the borderland—from the University of San Diego, twenty miles away from the U.S./Mexico border crossing. This precise context likely refers us to this metaphor of the borderlands which is a "betwixt and between" liminal area—a zone that straddles heightened conflict, mismatched commerce, multilingual urbanity, and transnational movements. Embodying power relations, border zones imply access for some, elusiveness for others. Borderlands are distant and distinct from mainstream culture yet intrinsically a part of them. A politico-geographic borderland encompasses a set of physical entry points, notions of legality/illegality and citizenship, a sense of belonging/not belonging, patterns of migration, policing and enforcement, passing, permeability, and transgressions. In the social sciences, the trope of the borderland has been useful to theorize ideas about culture and more recently social justice (Calderon & Saldívar, 1991; Cantú, 2009; Naples, 2009; Rosaldo, 1989; Vila, 2000; 2003).

In this book, we use the "borderlands of education" as a metaphor for studying processes of educational exclusion in engineering and the social forces that create them. How is engineering a borderland discipline within academia? From our perspective, although privileged in some ways in society, engineering is in the borderlands of U.S. education. It is virtually absent from K–12 curriculum with important implications: simply, many youth are unaware of what engineers do and produce for society. Moreover, for college students, engineering courses are absent from the "core" or "general education" courses. This absence suggests that engineering is not important to one's broad base of knowledge. In what ways is engineering education permeable, malleable, and open to redefinition? Is there a "canon of engineering knowledge" that is shared and, if so, is it negotiable or fixed?

Who occupies space on these borderlands of engineering education? How is belonging interpreted and who are the outliers? Who are the social actors that "police" curricular structures in engineering education? In what ways do students migrate in and out of engineering majors? Does migration into the borderlands of engineering produce culture shock, and if so, for whom? Latinas in engineering education occupy intersecting borderlands. On the path to higher education, they face numerous societal obstacles resulting from a legacy of racism. As women, they are on the margins of the masculine space of engineering.

People occupying the borderlands can provide unique insights: "The words of the silenced shine a sometimes unflattering light on existing social and institutional structures and hierarchies of power that are invisible to those in the mainstream" (LeCompte, 1993 cited in Foor, Walden, and Trytten, 2007, p. 103). This book began as a case study of Latinas in engineering. Through their voices and experiences, we illuminate broader structural problems within engineering education. While most research has focused on how the efforts and individual characteristics of students need to change to ensure success in engineering, we ask, "How can engineering change and rise to the challenge of broadening participation?" Exploring this question and critically examining the borderlands of education allows us to pursue the potential for transformation with the goal of reconfiguring this space and transcending boundaries.

OVERVIEW OF THE BOOK

How is engineering an exclusionary culture? In Chapter 2, "Exclusionary Borderlands: Race, Gender, and Engineering Education," we consider the importance of the field of engineering and scrutinize the call for more diversity within engineering education. By examining how engineering and society co-construct one another, we highlight how technology is raced and gendered. It is within this context that students experience the climate of engineering education. We then investigate some of the problems of aggregation associated with studying these issues. Finally we conclude with a discussion of the structural problems of exclusion for Latinos and Latinas in education and the potential to recruit into engineering.

How do Latino/a students navigate engineering education? In Chapter 3, "Debunking the Myths: Trajectories of Latinas in Engineering," we closely examine quantitative data to illuminate trends among Latinos in engineering education. We begin by examining national data for intent to major in science and engineering. Then, using a comprehensive longitudinal data set, we report six-year graduation rates disaggregated by race/ethnicity and gender to show that recruitment is a more important issue than retention. We present data on engineering matriculants and analyze their six-year destinations. We highlight the engineering subdisciplines that Latinos and Latinas are most attracted to. Next, we consider transfer students since Latinos make up a large proportion of this important population. We review several features of successful Latino engineers including the effects of geography and institution type on academic persistence. We end the chapter by discussing remaining challenges for Latinas in engineering.

How do Latinas describe experiences of belonging in engineering education? In Chapter 4, "Voices of Latinas in Engineering," we draw on our qualitative research among Latina students to examine their experiences of the academic and social aspects of the climate of undergraduate engineering education. We describe "microaggressions" and use this framework in our analysis of how Latinas form counterspaces within the borderland of engineering education. This qualitative research, incorporating the rich, detailed perspectives through the women's voices, adds value to our understanding of the quantitative reality of engineering as a segregated space in academia.

What is the potential for radical change in engineering education? In Chapter 5, "Crossing Borders: Opportunities and Challenges," we review and propose strategies and practices that have the potential to diversify engineering. We re-envision engineering by proposing moving it from the border-lands into the core. We highlight innovative pedagogical strategies that could produce a more collaborative learning climate. We also consider the content of engineering and possibilities for change. Given the large number of Latinos who attend community college, we argue that engineering recruiting efforts in this context hold potential. Thus we also consider the important pathways of two-year institutions, including Hispanic-serving institutions (HSIs). Without precollege academic preparation, particularly in math and science, Latinas will be systematically disadvantaged from engineering. Expanding outreach is critical. As Latinas increasingly attend college, mentorship is key to helping Latinas choose engineering as a college major. There is a critical need to be increasingly focused on redefining engineering in ways that are meaningful to Latino youth.

Where do we go from here? In Chapter 6, "Conclusions," we summarize the main points of the book. We frame this work in the larger context of engineering and social justice. We propose the "Latino Engineering Paradox" as a missing element from the current discussion, which must be considered to make progress. We conclude with directions for future research in engineering education.

Chapter Two

Exclusionary Borderlands

Race, Gender, and Engineering Education

Is it worrisome that U.S. society produces a dwindling number of engineers? Why are there so few Latina engineers and what is the potential for change given demographic shifts of the Latino population? What are the structural problems of exclusion for Latinas in the borderlands of engineering education? There are diminishing numbers of engineering matriculants in undergraduate programs in the United States. Leaders have declared a crisis due to the decreasing pool of engineering degrees earned here. Given that women of all ethnicities attend college at higher rates than men, the conversations about engineering increasingly turn to how the discipline can be made more attractive to broader pools of potential participants. One recurring theme that emerges in the analysis of engineering's decline is the poor social and cultural environment of undergraduate engineering programs. Rather than attracting diverse students, engineering programs in higher education seem to repel students, notably women, Blacks, Latinos, and Native Americans. Scholars focus on the "climate" of engineering to understand the cultural characteristics of the discipline. A critical view of the future of engineering allows for scrutiny as to why the field is declining in popularity.

Engineering remains a borderland of education. Building on McIlwee and Robinson (1992), Foor, Walden, and Trytten (2007) assert that

> to be an engineer is to look like an engineer, talk like an engineer and act like an engineer. The process of becoming an engineer, as well as the being and doing of engineering, have a gendered, raced, and classed recent history: male, white, and privileged. (p. 105)

Another emerging body of work considers the roles of ability and disability (Moser, 2006; Sevo, 2011). In addition, researchers have recently begun to explore the heteronormativity (Cech & Waidzunas, 2011) and sexuality as axes of difference among engineers (Riley & Pawley 2011).

Gender, race, class, sexuality, and ability are central organizing principles that are embedded in how technology is generated, disseminated, and appropriated. Although we acknowledge the importance of the multiple dimensions of inequity, in this book, we focus primarily on gender and race/ethnicity. How does an academic discipline, seemingly involved with neutral objectives, bear gender and race? The field of engineering is intimately tied to a social history that evolved in a particular set of ways in concert with our societal problems and progress. To argue that engineering, or any discipline for that matter, is value-free, neutral, and objective is a myth. And yet while most academic disciplines in the United States shifted after the women's rights movements, drawing in a wider pool of participants that shaped intellectual trajectories, in the social landscape of engineering, relatively fewer women were drawn in. Today the pool of participants is staggeringly homogenous and slow to change compared with the once similarly stratified professions of law, medicine, and business that have achieved wider heterogeneity.

In this chapter, we consider the importance of the field of engineering. By examining how engineering and society co-construct one another, we highlight how technology is raced and gendered. We argue engineering itself is a gendered and raced space that structures hierarchies, establishes norms, and standardizes practices. The rigid borders of engineering were built through a history of exclusion that continues to shape its social context today. It is within this context that students experience the climate of engineering education. We scrutinize the call for more diversity within engineering education. We then investigate some of the problems of aggregation associated with studying these issues. We discuss concepts and terminology including *race*, *ethnicity*, *Latino*, and *Hispanic*. Finally we conclude with a discussion of the structural problems of exclusion for Latinos and Latinas in education and the potential to recruit them into engineering.

ENGINEERING AS A SOCIETAL KEYSTONE

The 20th century included remarkable engineering innovations: electrification, automobiles, airplanes, water distribution, agricultural mechanization, computers, telephones, refrigeration, spacecraft, Internet, imaging, radio and television, laser and fiber optics, and a tremendous proliferation of structural constructions including large dams, skyscrapers, and bridges (National Academy of Engineering, 2009). Electrification alone was responsible for unprecedented economic development, transforming rural and urban areas and changing everyday mechanisms of subsistence. From the micro household level to the macro industrial, from small appliances to international telecommunication networks that link us all, these changes have had profound effects on society. The work of engineers has propelled globalization by effectively shrinking our world, as we connect to more places without physically leaving our environments and watch change happen across the world via televised satellite images (National Academy of Engineering, 2009). Juan Lucena (2005), an engineer and expert in science and technology studies, asserts that the large-scale international problems addressed by the science and engineering communities have been intimately tied with politics and policy making in the United States: "Due to the increasing importance of science and technology in all areas of American life, the making of scientists and engineers has become a significant governmental act to ensure national security, economic growth, and sometimes social well-being" (Lucena, 2005, p. 5). Just as technology has had a profound effect on us, the U.S. government has had a profound effect on technology.

How have ideas of "progress" based on economic growth and societal well-being differently affected and differentially benefited diverse groups? Social scientists lend a critical eye to the concept of progress. The material manifestations of projects designed to "modernize" society have long been imbued with an uncomplicated sense that progress uniformly improves the welfare of all. Ideas of progress and modernization, however, go hand in hand with power relations, defining who is civilized and who is "backward," and constructing notions of citizenship, belonging, and race. While engineering does much to advance basic human needs, such as potable water, in some cases, it can exacerbate the differences between the "haves" and "have-nots." How and against whom will weapons be deployed? Which communities will freeways divide? Where and what function will surveillance cameras serve?

SOCIAL CONTEXT OF ENGINEERING

> Researchers in the social sciences and humanities . . . will fail to understand our societies if they do not take into account the role of technology and science. . . . Engineers and scientists . . . will fail to build well-functioning technological systems if they do not take into account that these systems are embedded in society. (Bijker, 2012, p. 625)

Here we share three examples to highlight how broader societal conditions influence technical developments which, in turn, affect society:

1. Both the mother and wife of eminent inventor and engineer Alexander Graham Bell were deaf, leading Bell to want to experiment with acoustics and elocution to produce telephone technology (Bruce,

1990). Bell received many accolades and honorary degrees during his lifetime. Many years later, early pioneers of cell phone technology worked at Bell Labs (namesake of the inventor), to develop the antecedents to our modern-day mobile phones (Farley, 2007).

2. Actor Hedy Lamarr, after divorcing an Austrian arms dealer in the 1940s, invented frequency-hopping technology to serve the U.S. war effort (Rhodes, 2011). Her invention was patented by the Navy and classified as top secret, and would later be used as the precursor for wireless technologies today (cell networks, Bluetooth, global positioning systems [GPS]). Lamarr, however, for years was only recognized as "the most beautiful woman in the world" and was not recognized for her contributions to science until the 1990s, by which time the patent had already expired (upon receiving the news, the actor, then in her late 80s, exclaimed, "Well, it's about time!").

3. Bertha Benz, wife of Karl Benz (of the first patented automobile), was honored at age 95 for her societal contribution as the first person to drive an automobile over a long distance (Bertha Benz Memorial Club e.V, n.d.). Although as an unmarried woman she was one of the initial investors in Karl Benz's automobile project, after she married him, she lost her legal right to participate. Without telling her husband and without permission of the authorities, in 1888, Bertha Benz drove a record 66 miles, claiming to want to visit her mother to demonstrate to both her husband and the broader public that such an achievement was feasible (a local pharmacy served as the first filling station).

These examples highlight the gendered power relations involved in producing technological advancements. Bell, a White man, enjoyed privileges such as credibility and an overwhelming number of accolades and honorary degrees, and continues to be celebrated. Lamarr and Benz, though privileged as White and upper class, were not considered credible because they were women, and remain essentially unrecognized for their contributions.

Nonetheless, the examples of Bell, Lamarr, and Benz illustrate that our experiences with our social world powerfully shape the developments and advances of technology. Similarly, engineering and technology powerfully shape society. Scholars of science, technology, and society (STS) term this process: *co-constructive* (Bijker & Law, 1994; Faulkner, 2001; Lohan, 2000; Pritchard, 2011). Technology and society are *mutually constituting*. To illustrate this point, one could consider the dramatic changes in modes of communication, both designs and uses, in the first decade of the 21st century. We can also see this co-construction in a more physical sense in examples of how gender embodies technological advances. Consider breast implants, prosthetic devices, and physical contraceptive technology, among many others, to examine how technology physically changes women. Similarly, men are increasingly subjects of technological embodiment, from hair transplants to pectoral implants to penile dysfunction technology, complicating categories of gender, sexuality, age, and others. The field of study devoted to understanding the embodiment of technology is called cyborgology (Haraway, 1987; 1996). The application of STS frameworks to engineering is an area of current interest, and scholars are building on the intellectual domain of STS to explore engineering (Davidow, 2012; Faulkner, 2007; Pawley, 2007; Phipps, 2007; Tonso, 2007).

Researchers are increasingly critically examining power relations within productions of technology, specifically, how technology shapes race, class, and gender and vice versa. While engineering and technological advances may appear to be value-free, they are enmeshed within a framework of power. For example, the now infamous Long Island overpasses were designed with an unusually low height specification of "as little as nine feet of clearance at the curb" (Winner, 1980, p. 123). Historian Robert A. Caro (1974) compellingly documents this structural peculiarity, attributing this outcome to the social-class and racist biases of their designer, Robert Moses. Langdon Winner uses this example in his renown article *Do Artifacts Have Politics?*, asserting

> that the two hundred or so low-hanging overpasses on Long Island were deliberately designed to achieve a particular social effect. . . . Automobile-owning whites of "upper" and "comfortable middle" classes . . . would be free to use the parkways for recreation and commuting . . . [while] poor people and blacks, who normally used public transit, were kept off the roads because the twelve-foot tall buses could not get through the overpasses. (Winner, 1980, pp. 123–124)

In this example, we see that by structurally prohibiting access to racial minorities and low-income groups, the overpass itself reinscribes a racialized and class-stratified order with a lasting legacy. This example suggests that advances in technological engineering innovations are often deeply enmeshed within a broader field of power and politico-economic relations and co-construct societal configurations.

The 2012 controversy about the Microsoft patent popularly dubbed the "Ghetto App" is another example of how technology constructs race and reinforces class divisions. Microsoft does not refer to race in the title of their patent, "Pedestrian Route Production," nor does it use the term "ghetto" in its description. According to the patent, the objective is to take "the user through neighborhoods with violent crime statistics below a certain threshold" (Keyes, 2012). Proponents argue that such an application is simply "the next step in GPS technology" to send users a warning when they are about to enter an area deemed criminal (Keyes, 2012). Critics, by contrast, view this technological development as raced and classed (King, 2012). The term *ghetto* carries racial overtones conflated in our lexicon with "violent crime statis-tics" and neglects the social reality that crime is racialized due to profiling and other inequities in policing practices. The Ghetto App is an example of how power relations and, more specifically, *technological power* reinscribe society and can reinforce exclusion and segregation. The effect of such an app wields power to bear detrimental economic effects on communities of color by diverting pedestrian traffic away (Roberts, 2012). This case allows us to further probe the extent to which contemporary technological advances are designed for a specific social class and racial group (middle and White). Residents of the areas deemed "criminal" are also technology users, yet this application neglects this audience by constructing occupants of these neigh-borhoods as dangerous (for it is not the neighborhood itself that is criminal-ized; it is its inhabitants). In this example, we see that technology reinforces normative ideas about how society should engage with socio-geographic areas and people within them.

DEFICIT OF ENGINEERS: DWINDLING NUMBERS AND LACK OF DIVERSITY

The Bureau of Labor Statistics (BLS) predicts a deficit of engineers. They report that engineering employment opportunities are on the rise, but the number of engineering degrees awarded is projected to remain static (2011). Although engineering is an important part of the U.S. economy—in 2008, engineers held about 1.6 million jobs in the United States (BLS, 2011)—increasingly fewer U.S. undergraduate students are recruited into engineering education, especially women and underrepresented minorities (Jackson, 2004b; Congressional Commission on the Advancement of Women and Mi-norities in Science, Engineering and Technology Development (CAWM-SET), 2000). This problem will have deleterious effects on our nation's global leadership and on our society as a whole:

> The crisis stems from the gap between the nation's growing need for scientists, engineers, and other technically skilled workers, and its production of them. As the generation educated in the 1950s and 1960s prepares to retire, our colleges and universities are not graduating enough scientific and technical talent to step into research laboratories, software and other design centers, refineries, defense installations, science policy offices, manufacturing shop floors and high-tech startups. This "gap" represents a shortfall in our national scientific and technical capabilities. (Jackson, 2004b, p.1)

While the numbers of engineering degrees have expanded abroad, they have declined in the United States. Leaders in U.S. engineering communities express alarm over the shortfall of well-prepared engineers. According to the published forecasts of the future of engineering, if the issue of recruitment and retention of new engineering students is not addressed, technological and innovative capabilities will dwindle (arguably) resulting in the greatest challenge to America's prosperity (National Academy of Sciences, National Academy of Engineering, & Institute of Medicine of the National Academies, 2007). The social and economic ramifications of such stasis will thwart the development of many needed changes such as alternative technologies for sustainable energy use. In its report *Rising above the Gathering Storm: Energizing and Employing America for a Brighter Future*, the National Academy of Sciences asserts that at risk is

> the steady flow of knowledge and . . . the mechanism for converting information into the products and services that create jobs and improve the quality of modern life. Maintaining that vast and complex enterprise during an age of competition and globalization is challenging, but it is essential to the future of the United States. (National Academy of Sciences et al., 2007, p. 43)

Today, engineers are needed in a wide range of subdisciplines, and although some engineering demands can be filled with a global workforce, there is still a pressing need for on-site engineers in the United States to interact with clients and employees. New commercial and military air and spacecraft technologies provide jobs for aerospace engineers. Nuclear engineers are particularly in demand to develop nuclear power as an energy source, for new reactor designs, and to develop nuclear medical technology. Chemical engineers are needed for researching energy sources and to contribute to the developing fields of biotechnology and nanotechnology. The Department of Defense increasingly relies on engineers with security clearances to address national cybersecurity among many other issues. Biomedical engineers are needed to meet the health needs of our aging society, particularly to develop more cost-efficient and technologically effective medical devices and equipment. Mechanical engineers are needed for product design across a wide range of commodities, including cars, heating, ventilation, consumer products, and building more efficient energy sources. As our population grows, civil engineers are needed to meet the demands required for the expansion of transportation, water supply, and environmental control systems. Electrical engineers are increasingly needed for wireless technological advances, transmitters, navigation systems, electric power generators, and applications for high-density batteries. And industrial engineers are needed to make products cheaper, better, and faster.

A post-9/11 climate intensified the call for engineers. Only two years after 9/11, the National Science Foundation (NSF) had funded "$20 million worth of exploratory research and education programs dealing with terrorism" (Lucena, 2005). Prominent engineering publications outlining the future of the field continue to highlight the importance of developing new technologies to address homeland security and the role of engineering innovations in preventing terrorist threats. For example, in *The Quiet Crisis: Falling Short in Producing American Scientific and Technical Talent*, Shirley Jackson, president of the Rensselaer Polytechnic Institute, asserts that the "gap" between our technical needs as a nation and the paucity of new professionals in science, technology, engineering, and mathematics (STEM) has become a problem of national security:

> The need to make the nation safer from emerging terrorist threats that endanger the nation's people, infrastructure, economy, health, and environment, makes this gap all the more critical and the need for action all the more urgent. We ignore this gap at our peril. Closing it will require a national commitment to develop more of the talent of all our citizens, especially the under-represented majority—the women, minorities, and persons with disabilities who comprise a disproportionately small part of the nation's science, engineering, and technology workforce. (2004a, p. 1)

In a speech addressing *New Ideas to Advance STEM Education in the U.S.* at the Brookings Institute on September 12, 2011, acting secretary of commerce Rebecca Blank (Blank, 2011) exhorted:

> Our competitiveness as a nation depends upon our success. America will have a difficult time competing for 21st century industries if our children lack the skills and the education that are integral to those industries in the future. Make no mistake: this is a national imperative and a national economic imperative. It's critical that we understand and treat it as one. That's why this administration is so strongly committed to doing its share to strengthening STEM training in the U.S. Ultimately, it's part of how we rebuild America's economic foundation stronger than it was before the recent financial crisis.

Such sentiments in the past decade have resulted in numerous legislative policy recommendations. These include, for example, the American Competitiveness Initiative, introduced by President George W. Bush in 2006, calling for increases in federal funding for support in educational development in STEM fields. A Committee on Science, Engineering, and Public Policy, through the U.S. National Academies, also expressed concern about the declining state of STEM education in the United States and developed recommendations for improving America's talent pool and strengthening teacher training in science, math, and technology (2007). The NSF funds important research projects related to STEM education, many of which incorporate dissemination efforts to reach students and teachers and impact programming efforts. These efforts, significantly, amounted to important policy as of August 9, 2007, with the America COMPETES Act, or "America Creating Opportunities to Meaningfully Promote Excellence in Technology, Education, and Science" Act, which provided funding for investments in education and research, and represents at a federal level the importance of providing greater infrastructure for development in STEM fields including transferring of knowledge from those retiring to a new workforce (America COMPETES Act, 2007). In 2010, the America COMPETES Act was reauthorized, resulting in continued funding with modest increases for the NSF (Library of Congress, 2010).

According to the Economic and Statistics Administration calculations from the U.S. Census data, in 2009, there were 2,079,000 engineering jobs held by men compared with 330,000 engineering jobs held by women (Beede, Julian, Langdon, McKittrick, Khan, & Doms, 2011). Women held only 14% of all engineering jobs in the United States. This represents a 1% increase since data were available in 2000. What is daunting about these numbers is that among all college-educated workers in the United States, that is, among the entire pool, women represent 49%. Alarmingly, women in engineering represent a huge gap. Among all workers, both college educated and non–college educated, women represent 48%. This is an era in history in which women are, overall, not excluded from the workforce in general. Rather, women are attending and graduating from college at the highest historical rates, and this is represented in their share of the labor force. In the case of engineering, however, the data indicate an enormous gender gap (Beede et al., 2011). While women are making gains with jobs in the physical and life sciences steadily over time (with women representing about 40% of those positions as of 2009), the numbers for women in engineering are comparatively abysmal.

Although White male students vastly outnumber all other groups in engineering education, increasingly fewer White men are choosing engineering. Additionally, current engineering professionals many of whom are part of the baby boom generation are retiring, leaving even more gaps open in engineering industries. Leaders call this situation a "crisis" and are devising recommendations for change (Jackson, 2004b; America COMPETES Act, 2007; CAWMSET, 2000). According to these sources, it is critical to devote resources and create policies to rectify this problem in higher education. Efforts have been initiated in government, industrial, and educational sectors. The 2013 budget for the White House Office of Science and Technology includes a "world class commitment" for science, engineering, and research (ASEE, 2012b). In 2012, President Obama met with deans of engineering programs at an American Society of Engineering Education (ASEE) conference to indicate his active support (ASEE, 2012a). Such initiatives signal that the field is ripe for change.

Beyond the shortfall of engineers, there is a pressing need for greater diversity in engineering. Decades ago, President Carter affirmed the need for STEM to appeal to a more diverse population in the Science and Engineering

Equal Opportunity Act of 1980, which also gave the NSF a congressional mandate to pursue diversity in STEM fields (Malcolm, Chubin, & Jesse, 2004). Diversity among engineers produces a wider range of innovative products that take into consideration race and gender. Margolis and Fisher provide provocative examples in their landmark study, *Unlocking the Club-house*:

> Some early voice-recognition systems were calibrated to typical male voices. As a result women's voices were literally unheard. . . . Similar cases are found in many other industries. For example, a predominantly male group of engineers tailored the first generation of automotive airbags to adult male bodies, resulting in avoidable deaths in women and children. (2002, pp. 2–3)

Would such technological deficiencies have been detected with a more diverse group of engineers? As Jackson declares,

> If we engage the talent—with its beauty and the beautiful minds—of all of our young people in science and engineering studies and professions—we will address our national self-interest. And, we will have acknowledged the value inherent in talent and inherent in diversity. (Jackson, 2004a, p. 72)

To summarize, the crisis of dwindling numbers of students entering engineering represents a critical problem for the future of the field. Fewer White men, historically the largest group in engineering, and others are choosing engineering upon matriculation. Furthermore, the lack of women and underrepresented minorities in engineering creates a social context that is grossly stratified by race and gender. It is essential to have wide representation in engineering considering its centrality in shaping society, the influential role that engineering leaders play in selecting which projects are valued and funded, and the possible ethical implications for both.

BORDERLANDS IN ENGINEERING: CULTURAL CLIMATE

Researchers in engineering education attribute the low representation of women and underrepresented minorities to contextual factors, such as the current institutional climate within engineering education programs and a history of rigidity in the engineering curriculum. The effects of both continue to shape the current context, resulting in one of the last segregated spaces in academia. The climate in engineering for women has been described as "chilly" rather than warm and welcoming. Lord's narrative in Chapter 1 provides an anecdotal form of evidence of how this chilliness manifests. While change in academia occurs incrementally, researchers continue to describe the field as exclusionary (Camacho & Lord, 2013; Godfrey, 2007; Godfrey & Parker, 2010; Tonso, 2006; 2007).

Exclusionary Culture of Engineering

With its roots in the military-industrial complex, the rigidity of the engineering curriculum was designed to ideologically "keep men in line" and the reputation of rigor continues to be prized (Hacker, 1989). The institutional character of engineering education is notoriously inflexible and the legacy of this rigidity persists. Engineering has the most extensive prerequisites of any major, with a strict template of required courses that must be taken in the first year of study. Students must take math, chemistry, and physics beginning their first year in college to be able to take subsequent engineering courses; these prerequisites require students to make decisions about their major early in their college career. The lack of exploratory, elective-like courses prevents potential new majors from dabbling in, or trying out, the major—a possibility in many other disciplines. Students interested in engineering must make decisions earlier than those in other majors. Many engineering students have few or no free electives. One consequence of the rigidity of the curriculum and lack of elective possibilities is that few students migrate into the field (Ohland, Sheppard, Lichtenstein, Eris, Chachra, & Layton, 2008). Competency in calculus or physics is not required in the core curriculum at many universities. As a result, a student who decides to major in engineering after the first year is at a disadvantage since he or she must still complete the first-year courses, typically extending graduation by a year. The narrow inbound pathway is a distinct feature of engineering (Ohland et al., 2008, p. 275).

The total female population in engineering continues to be staggeringly low, even though fields such as business, medicine, and law have achieved near gender parity (Bradley, 2000; Sanoff, 2005). For example, in 2009, White women received only 11.6% of all engineering undergraduate degrees, despite the fact that women surpass men in college enrollments. Among underrepresented minorities in engineering (Latino, Black, and Native American men and women), the total percentage of undergraduate degrees awarded was only about 14% (NSF, 2009a). The numbers of women and minority faculty in engineering education continue to be abysmal (see Chapter 3).

Systematic exclusionary forces have carved engineering into an elite academic enclave. Amy Slaton's groundbreaking historical analysis of the racialized power relations in engineering education illustrates the legacy of this process on African Americans (Slaton, 2010). It is important to note that the history of exclusion differs for women, Latinos, African Americans, Native Americans, and Asian Americans in engineering education. Studies have shown that the underrepresentation of minorities is a problem shared by all majors (American Council on Education, 2006; National Center for Education Statistics, 2000) while underrepresentation of women is a problem unique to engineering and computer science (Lord et al., 2009). Before 1952, women were not allowed admission in engineering, particularly at institutes of technology, and later they were "oddities at best, outcasts at worst, defying traditional gender norms" (Bix, 2004, p. 27). The exclusion of ethnic minorities in engineering can be understood through the broader lens of educational inequities. In K–12 schools, college preparatory courses were racially segregated and many Latino students were tracked into vocational programs; fewer received educational opportunities including access to college counseling. Although the 1964 Federal Civil Rights Act bars discrimination by sex and race, it did little to dramatically change the culture of engineering. One possible explanation for this may be the omnipresence of White male leadership (see Chapter 3, Table 3.6). Numerous publications have documented an engineering culture pointing not only to issues of "climate" but also to the lack of role models, rigid pedagogical approaches that lack creative design elements and teamwork, and even subtle habits used to establish who belongs in engineering and who does not (Faulkner, 2007; Godfrey & Parker, 2010; Seymour & Hewitt, 1997; Tonso, 2007; see also Chapter 5). Today we can examine the gender and racial composition of students and faculty in engineering education to see that, structurally, many of the same challenges from thirty years ago acutely persist.

Because men make up 82% of those receiving engineering bachelor's degrees, a masculine homogeneity defines the character of engineering. Engineers' professional identities in the United States have historically been shaped by this hegemonic masculinity dating back to the 1890s (Frehill, 2004). Feminist studies of science and engineering argue that it is not enough to simply add women to increase the pool of women in engineering. Rather, engineering will be qualitatively different if women of all ethnicities are contributing to the conversations, taking on leadership positions, and collectively forging change. Men have shaped the discourse historically because of their overwhelming presence, and this has specifically affected the coproduction of gendered ideologies and engineering. According to science studies scholar Wendy Faulkner,

> Since gender is intricately interwoven with engineering, as it is with any other social institution, gender and engineering are co-produced or co-constructed. For example, the nerd stereotype is of men who are passionate about technology but a-social; the fact that these two are posited as mutually exclusive—to be technical is to be not-social—is one of the more powerful symbolic ways in which engineering appears gender inauthentic for women, given the strong association of women/femininities with caring about people. (2007, p. 334)

Although binaries are problematic analytically because they polarize a complex range of issues, feminist technology studies theorists' examination of an "easy-hard" binary, and the social construction of what it means for a discipline to be labeled "hard," offers insights into the reasons why women avoid technical careers. While engineering practice necessarily contains elements of both the technical and the social in designing products or processes that will be used by members of society, the technical is considered normative, while the social is often less visible—these distinctions map onto the dualism of technology as masculine and sociality as feminine (Faulkner, 2000, 2007). While this status quo is challenged internally (for example, by pedagogical innovators, formal structural interventions by institutions themselves and external agencies, and progressive individuals such as administrators, faculty, and students), glaring inequities for women and underrepresented minorities in engineering education indicate that engineering education is one of the few remaining segregated academic spaces.

Women's exclusion from and fragmented participation within technical fields has more to do with culture than aptitude, skill, or interest. For example, the "Rosie the Riveter" campaign was used by the U.S. government in World War II to fill jobs with women when men left during the wartime effort. The historical event of recruiting women into formerly male-dominated jobs resulted in many women learning technical skills to meet factory labor demands (Milgram, 2011). Women worked assiduously and were praised for their "patriotic duty"; however, after World War II ended and men returned home, the rhetoric changed. Women holding "men's jobs" were told they were no longer needed. It is clear, retrospectively, that women's contributions were seen as an extension of their service roles. Many women of color had long worked in menial jobs and been treated as second-class citizens. When middle-class White women were similarly treated as a disposable workforce, and told to go home after learning valuable technical skills, their labor contributions were devastatingly devalued on a societal level. Whereas this historical moment presented an opportunity to normalize the role of women in technical fields as legitimate contributors, instead, it reinscribed a male hegemonic social order where women were once again shut out.

Although women have made some gains in technical fields, there has been backlash. An extreme example is the atrocity of the 1989 Montreal massacre, in which women engineering students were murdered by an irate gunman targeting them as "feminists." This is a haunting reminder of the loathing toward women in engineering. Racism and sexism, endemic in the culture of engineering, are not recognized as such. Rather, as Riley describes in her book *Engineering and Social Justice* (2008), too often the "problem" of few people of color in engineering is narrowly constructed as one only of "underrepresentation." Riley explores the long history of sexism in engineering education and workplace culture and argues for redefining the problem by confronting the underlying racism and stereotypes in engineering culture.

Because engineering constructs itself as "value neutral" or "objective" without recognizing these as social constructions, "engineering has reflected some unjust biases embedded in our social structures to the point where they become so mainstream as to be invisible. This default set of values has been inculcated in engineers through the engineering education process" (Riley, 2008, p. 96). Scholars have begun to examine structural inequities in engineering and science education in greater depth, particularly for African Americans (Lewis, 2003; Mutegi, 2011; Slaton, 2010). Methodological advances have also revealed systematic measurement biases that have historically clouded researchers' analysis of small populations such as underrepresented groups in engineering (Ohland et al., 2011). More research is needed to examine opportunity structures that will overcome these inherent biases and barriers, and to create democratic and equitable educational systems (Slaton, 2011).

Internalizing a Negative Climate

Women continue to face subtle but persistent instances of gender bias in the college classroom. These involve many factors including sexist language, few female role models, exclusion from study groups and work teams, low numbers of women students, and academic competition rather than cooperation fostered by professors (Camacho, Lord, Brawner, & Ohland, 2010; Hanson, 1997; National Council for Research on Women, 2001; Rosser, 1993; Seymour & Hewitt, 1997). A three-year study of enrollment patterns and interview responses of 460 students on seven diverse campuses by Seymour and Hewitt (1997) revealed reasons students leave STEM majors after they enroll in college and helped explain the underrepresentation of women in these fields. They conclude that women students experience the discipline very differently from men, thus partially explaining why they leave. They suggest that women's experiences can be improved by helping them gain better coping skills, fostering their relationships with other women in their disciplines, hiring more women faculty, and providing more female role models and mentors, all of which contribute to a more comfortable climate. More recent work by Margolis and Fisher (2002) in the field of computing revealed similar findings.

According to the Women in Engineering Programs Advocacy Network (WEPAN) Pilot Climate Survey (Brainard, Metz, & Gillmore, 2000) of more than 8,000 undergraduate engineering students at 29 different colleges and universities, there are significant differences in the way males and females experience educational climate at their institutions. Women reported being less confident in their abilities, more overwhelmed by the fast pace and the heavy workload, less comfortable asking questions in class, and less certain that engineering was the right major for them than did their male counterparts. In our research on engineering climate among over 1,500 students, compared with men, women reported different perceptions of fairness, less of a sense of belonging, and problems with issues of diversity (Camacho, Lord, Brawner, & Ohland, 2010). According to Adelman's study of men and women in engineering, women tend to report higher degrees of dissatisfaction with their program than male students. He found that the women who left engineering did not do so because of poor grades, but rather because of environmental factors (Adelman, 1998). The fast pace and feelings of being overloaded were identified as factoring into their decision to leave.

Given the low numbers of women and particularly Latinas in engineering education, there are not enough faculty or students to achieve what has been termed a "critical mass." This concept suggests that a sufficient number of individuals inspires a collective action that is somehow different than that of a single individual (Oliver, Marwell, & Teixeira, 1985). Most of this research has been done on women in leadership positions in industry. For example, in a study of "token" women in a corporation, Kanter observed that gender stereotyping accompanies the presence of one or two women in a department and concluded that hiring women in clusters of at least three was needed (Kanter, 1977). Etzkowitz and colleagues place this threshold at 15% (Etzkowitz, Kemelgor, Neuschatz, Uzzi, & Alonzo, 1994). For faculty, researchers recommend a critical mass of at least three women in an academic department (Etzkowitz, Kemelgor, Neuschatz, & Uzzi, 1994). More research is needed to explore the concept of critical mass for women in engineering education, particularly work that is of an intersectional nature that also considers the race/ethnicity of the women. As Chapter 3 indicates, the paucity of women faculty role models is a significant problem in most engineering programs nationwide.

Women who are successful in science and engineering in academia face discrimination throughout their careers (Rosser, 2012). In reviewing the climate studies of 19 U.S. universities that have received NSF ADVANCE grants, researchers found "that as compared to men, the women on science and engineering faculties perceive the internal climate at their universities as more disrespectful, noncollegial, sexist, individualistic, competitive, nonsupportive, intolerant of diversity, and nonegalitarian" (Bilimoria, Joy, & Liang, 2008). These are the responses and attitudes of PhD women who have successfully persisted through the engineering pipeline and achieved the highest level of education in their fields. These data suggest that even after securing a tenure track position, and achieving some equity with men, women professors in science and engineering continue to perceive the environment as hostile, unwelcoming, and difficult.

Institutional norms, social barriers, and environmental factors contribute to the underrepresentation of women in engineering fields and to the systematic exclusion of girls from a young age (c.f. Hill, Corbett, & St. Rose, 2010). Although many people believe that bias against women in STEM is no longer a problem, research shows that the problem is complex and intertwined with societal assumptions and associations regarding gender roles. Biases against women and girls pervade our culture, and are reproduced by both men and women. In an afterschool Lego class in 2009, for example, a six-year-old girl was excitedly describing one of her Christmas presents when a six-year-old boy said, "You can't have a Lego dump truck because you are a girl! You must have a *dumb* truck" (K. W. Lord, personal communication, January, 2009). Already biases are enacted by age six. Although most people would not directly support the stereotype that girls are not as good as boys in math and science, the dominance of males in science and math occupations contributes to unconscious associations for "male: science" and "female: non-science." This unconscious or "implicit bias," as it has been called by researchers (https://implicit.harvard.edu), helps explain how people end up unintentionally perpetuating stereotypes. There has been a large amount of research on implicit bias and specifically its relevance for women and science (Nosek, Banaji, & Greenwald, 2002; Nosek et al., 2009). Such implicit biases may contribute to steering young women from science and engineering, influence adults' decisions to encourage or discourage their daughters from pursuing STEM careers, and influence employers' hiring decisions and evaluations of female employees.

For students, stereotype threat research indicates that students have a tendency to act in accordance with expectations, both implicit and explicit (Smith, DiTomaso, Farris, & Cordero, 2001; Steele, 1997; Steele, Spencer, & Aronson, 2002). Individuals operating under a "stereotype threat" (i.e., "girls are not as good at math or science as boys") often self-fulfill the stereotype by rereading items more often and working slower with less accuracy. The threat can be induced easily by asking students to indicate their gender before a test or having a larger ratio of men to women in a testing situation. Women face stereotype threat in engineering (Kilgore, Shepard, Atman, & Chachra, 2011). Latinas face the double threat of ethnic and gender stereotypes (Gonzales, Blanton, & Williams, 2002). This theory suggests that the earliest messages young girls receive in math and science classes, important fields for STEM majors, are critical. When girls and boys are told they will perform at equal levels, and that they possess equal skills, the gender gap is erased. Raising awareness of stereotype threat for students, parents, and teachers can help to minimize its effects. There is considerable research on combating the effects of stereotype threat (Singletary, Rugs, Hebl, & Davies, 2009) including work specifically focused on college women in STEM (Miyake, Kost-Smith, Finkelstein, Pollock, Cohen, & Ito, 2010) although this is not familiar to most engineering educators.

STUDYING ENGINEERING EDUCATION:
PROBLEMS OF AGGREGATION

Over the past two decades, feminists of color have argued for a more nuanced and differentiated understanding of gender, asserting that "women" and "men" are not monolithic groups and that experiences by gender cannot be understood outside of a wider prism of difference that accounts for both race and social class among other categories. Feminists of color have long understood that their specific positionality within academia cannot be understood simply through a single societal organizing principle such as gender, race, social class, or sexual orientation. Black feminist Patricia Hill Collins was a pioneer in articulating the concept of "intersectionality" to describe how women's identities converge (1986, 1990, 2000, 2006). That is, women of color hold memberships in multiple social groups, and individual identities result from these multiple experiences. The term was coined by legal scholar Kimberlé Crenshaw (1989) to describe how identities and lived experiences converge in multidimensional ways. Current debates among feminist theorists question whether intersectionality is a methodology or a theory (see for example Davis, 2008) and criticize how a framework of intersectionality falls short of examining intracultural-gendered differences (c.f. Nash, 2008; Walcott, 2005) and their "interferences" (Moser, 2006). Here we incorporate its use to counter the dominant narrative in the engineering education literature that constructs marginal groups as undifferentiated collectives—combining all women into a single category (as a minority group) and all people of color into another single category (as non-White) as a mode of making visible that which is often invisible (see also Crenshaw, 2011).

In the context of engineering education, much knowledge stands to be gained using an intersectional lens to understand the social conditions that differently attract men and women to engineering, and to understand the factors that influence their retention in STEM fields. Research in STEM education tends to conflate racial/ethnic categories, aggregating and constructing a category called, "minorities." Disaggregation for social analysis, particularly in STEM higher education, is often difficult by discipline, because of the low population numbers. Much nuance, however, is lost in the aggregation of social groups. A notable example of the power of a single individual's story is the work of Foor, Walden, and Trytten (2007) who described in depth the story of female, multi-minority engineering student from a socioeconomically disadvantaged background. This rich, deep ethnography of one student provides "a microphone for the voices of the marginalized to be heard" (Foor, Walden, & Trytten, 2007, p. 113). In a similar methodological vein, Riley and Pawley (2011) explore the experiences of a lesbian Latina engineering minor to critique myths of gender and race in engineering education.

In general, there is a paucity of disaggregated data on underrepresented groups, especially women of color, in STEM. Most studies aggregate by group, for example considering "women" or "underrepresented minorities," thereby assuming all women or all African Americans and Latinos share the same educational experiences. Because there are deep limitations to using a single category of analysis, feminists suggest the need to use an intersectional approach to best understand the multiple positions that combine unique gendered, racialized, social class, and sexuality perspectives that individuals inhabit. An intersectional approach does not gloss over differences; rather, such an approach considers that not all women, for example, share the same experiences. A White woman, for example, as a member of a dominant majority group, may experience sexism; a Black woman may experience racism and sexism. Thus an intersectional approach accounts for the axes of privilege and disadvantage. The core of the intersectional paradigm suggests that relations of power are central in defining identities, and that identities may shift.

Similarly, many excellent studies also aggregate by field combining science, technology, engineering, and mathematics into STEM (Seymour & Hewitt, 1997; Hill, Corbett, & St. Rose, 2010), to the exclusion of studying a single discipline in depth. While there are important methodological and theoretical arguments for aggregating these fields (because of shared foundational course requirements, or because of historical similarities in these disciplines), there are also disadvantages. Aggregating by discipline can lead to hollow findings due to a lack of specificity. Glossing over differences buries diverse intracultural differences by discipline, leading to a silencing of voices that ultimately hampers our ability to understand the social positions of those on the border in engineering education. Engineering education is uniquely different from other categories aggregated in STEM. For example, participation of women is significantly less in engineering than in biology or chemistry or mathematics. Most people have minimal or no exposure to what engineering really is unless they know someone who is an engineer. Although science is standard in K–12 curricula, engineering as a discipline is not. National polls have shown that the public has less favorable opinions of engineers than scientists, believing engineers are less likely to be engaged in the community or to play a role in saving lives (National Academy of Engineering, 2008). See Chapter 5 for a discussion of engineering as a borderland discipline in academia.

Members of minority student groups differ based on group histories, geographic region, social class backgrounds, and, of course, gender. Within predominately White colleges and universities, sometimes students of color coalesce and forge alliances because they share similar experiences of discrimination, marginalization, or exclusion. This is, in fact, how some groups with very different backgrounds, came to share a common pan-ethnic identity. For example, the category "Asian" melds together distinct groups with very different social histories; second generation Hmong immigrants to the United States, for example, share little in common with Japanese Americans. To dominant populations in the United States, however, these groups are perceived as racially and culturally similar. Even though they may have little in common, the dominant perception reifies their identities. The historically invented category (and pejorative term) "Oriental" is based on Eurocentric notions of how different, or exotic, the East appeared when compared with the West. The category Asian was created by activist members of these distinct groups as a form of ethnic solidarity (LeEspiritu, 1992).

CATEGORIZING IDENTITIES: LATINO AND HISPANIC

The category of "Hispanic" is a U.S. construct and represents an amalgamation of various national backgrounds that share the Spanish language. The term was created by the U.S. Census in the 1980s using an English adaptation of the word "Hispano" (which means Spanish). For some people, the term Hispanic is problematic due to its origins and reference to colonial Spain. In the United States, the term "Latino" is sometimes used interchangeably with Hispanic, although some prefer Latino because it more directly refers to Latin American origins and suggest a shared heritage of indigenous peoples and colonizers shaped by conquest. Preferences in identification are sometimes influenced by geography and political affiliation. Note that Hispanic or Latino is considered by the U.S. Census to be an ethnicity not a race and groups categorized as Hispanic or Latino are racially diverse. According to the most recent U.S. Census,

> The terms "Hispanic" or "Latino" refer to persons who trace their origin or descent to Mexico, Puerto Rico, Cuba, Spanish-speaking Central and South American countries, and other Spanish cultures. Origin can be considered as the heritage, nationality group, lineage, or country of the person or the person's parents or ancestors before their arrival in the United States. People who identify their origin as Hispanic or Latino may be of any race. (U.S. Census Bureau, 2012a)

The category Hispanic is set apart on the U.S. census as the only ethnic group listed and respondents must designate whether they are or are not Hispanic. Separately, they are instructed to choose the race that best fits them from among "Black or African American, American Indian or Alaska Native, Asian, Native Hawaiian or Other Pacific Islander, White, or Some Other Race" (Humes, Jones, & Ramirez, 2011). Interestingly, in the 2010 Census, about 37% of those who marked "Hispanic or Latino" as their ethnicity chose "some other race" (Humes et al., 2011). This might suggest a discomfort with the specific racial categories the census presents. Despite the fact that some Latinos categorize themselves as White on the census, many face discrimination based on skin color. Skin pigmentation among Latinos in the United States varies widely. Racialization for Latinos is a result of the long U.S. racial order based on Black-White differences. According to Frank, Akresh, and Lu, "Most Latino immigrants recognize the advantages of a White racial designation when asked to self-identify, but wider society is not often accepting of this White expansion" (2010, p. 378).

Categories of race and ethnicity are messy because both are social constructions (not biological facts). They change often over time, are grounded in historical power relations, and often shape social relations involving inclusivity and exclusivity. Although the census makes this distinction between race and ethnicity for Hispanics, in our work, following the recommendation of the American Anthropological Association (1997), we conflate race/ethnicity. This is how the terms are popularly understood and used. Some sociologists use the term "ethnoracial" to capture such usage (Nunn, 2011). "For Latinos, efforts to consider race as distinct from ethnicity often miss the actual ways that individuals understand boundaries between groups" (Frank, Akresh, & Lu, 2010, p. 379). Although problematic, the categories of race and ethnicity are relevant to us as researchers because they are the products of a socio-legal system and continue to reflect power relations that define society. For Latinos, these terms are important not only as signifiers of people's individual identities. More importantly, in examining structural problems of education, these categories provide data that can be used to study groups that continue to be marginalized due to a historical legacy that has shaped patterns of migration and diaspora, refugee and economic status, segregation, educational opportunities, labor, poverty, and the unequal distribution of wealth. "It is important to recognize the categories to which individuals have been assigned historically in order to be vigilant about the elimination of discrimination" (American Anthropological Association, 1997).

HETEROGENEITY OF LATINOS

Latinos are a heterogeneous group, with distinct migratory and sociopolitical histories resulting in variation in educational experiences. The census provides disaggregated data for the three largest Latino subgroups: Mexicans, Puerto Ricans, and Cubans. The data show variability in educational attainment for these three groups (U.S. Census Bureau, 2012b). In 2010, 26.2% of Cuban Americans attained a college degree, higher than all Hispanic subgroups; 10.6% of Mexican Americans and 17.5% of Puerto Ricans earned college degrees. Comparatively, 30.3% of Whites earned college degrees; 19.8% of Blacks and 52.4% of Asians earned a college degree.

The earliest waves of Cuban immigrants were political refugees, and were awarded special funds through the Migration and Refugee Assistance Act of 1962 and the Cuban Refugee Program, which provided financial assistance, resettlement costs, employment, and professional retraining courses for Cubans (Heller, 1972). These benefits explain, in part, the gap between Cubans and other Hispanic groups. Later waves of Cuban immigrants, however, were not granted the same benefits, resulting in segmentation among the social class statuses of Cubans in the United States.

Mexicans, by contrast, are economic immigrants, not political refugees, and the United States has formally and informally relied on Mexican labor since the beginning of the last century when the Dillingham Commission targeted them as a source of cheap labor in 1907 (Chavez, 1998). Mexican Americans have the lowest rates of educational attainment among Hispanics, for many reasons, including a history of segregated education (that persists because of poverty within neighborhoods), complicated by limited labor opportunities. The U.S. proximity to the Mexican border facilitated a relationship with undocumented workers, and Mexican workers engaged in settlement patterns in the United States as a result. Without systematic access to citizenship, the benefits of working legally and earning a fair wage in the United States eluded many Mexicans, with consequences for the larger Mexican American population (such as wider discrimination and the criminalization of all Mexicans, regardless of citizenship status). The so-called 1.5 generation (children born in Mexico but raised in the United States by their undocumented-worker parents) represents the betwixt status of students who face a constant discourse of exclusion by the media and society (Gonzales & Chavez, 2012).

Puerto Ricans are unique because of their status as American citizens after the Jones-Shafroth Act of 1917. The Puerto Rican educational system, however, is distinct from that in the United States. Because Puerto Rico is not a U.S. state, it is denied the same funding, resulting in educational discrepancies. Puerto Rico's historical status as a U.S. territory results in disenfranchisement for Puerto Ricans, who are unable to vote in U.S. congressional elections, yet have been subject to every U.S. compulsory draft. Emigration from Puerto Rico to the mainland also creates Puerto Rican ethnic enclaves in some U.S. cities. Puerto Ricans are concentrated in low-wage jobs and experience high poverty (Visser & Meléndez, 2011). Such structural dimensions affect the socioeconomic status of Puerto Ricans and partially explain their relatively lower levels of educational attainment.

LATINO EDUCATION: STRUCTURAL
PROBLEMS OF EXCLUSION

Despite the historical differences among Latino subgroups, U.S. Latino students may share experiences of discrimination because of classism and racism. According to Gándara and Contreras (2009), in their riveting book titled *The Latino Education Crisis*, Latino students share similarities in that many grow up in poor and dangerous neighborhoods where they attend impoverished schools. Many are raised in very low-income households with family members who may speak little English. Often their family members are undereducated. By the time Latino children reach kindergarten, they are behind on many academic measures. The cumulative effect of these disadvantages creates a higher high school dropout rate. Among Cubans, Mexicans, and Puerto Ricans, the total high school completion percentage in 2010 is 62.9%, compared with 87.6 % of Whites, 84.2% of Blacks and 88.9% of Asians (U.S. Census Bureau, 2012b). Researchers at the Urban Institute at Harvard, among others, assert that actual high school dropout rates are staggeringly lower than what is reported and some states have more egregious losses—some of this has been attributed to "No Child Left Behind" policies (Orfield, Losen, Wald, & Swanson, 2004). Nonetheless, Figure 2.1 shows the increase in high school graduation rates among Latinos in the United States longitudinally. Beginning in the 1990s, Latinas have higher high school graduation rates than Latino men (U.S. Census Bureau, 2012c).

Among all ethnic-gender group combinations in the United States, with the exception of Black men, there have been increasing rates of college graduation since the 1970s (U.S. Census Bureau, 2012c). Black men experienced a 0.3% dip in the last three years (between 2007 and 2010). About 30% of White men and women are graduating from college. By contrast, only about 15% of Latinas are college graduates, and 13% of Latinos are college graduates. The percentage of Latinos graduating from college has increased in the past forty years.

As shown in Figure 2.1, a gendered analysis of Latinos indicates that Latinas, beginning in 2005, have surpassed their male counterparts in college graduation. Saenz and Ponjuan (2009) found that Latino males are more likely to drop out of high school and enter the workforce rather than head to college. Of those who do enter college, increasingly higher rates of Latino men leave before graduating. This is particularly a problem for engineering because engineering attracts significantly more Latinos than Latinas. Low representation in engineering is conflated with the problem of "the vanishing Latino male in higher education" (Saenz & Ponjuan, 2009). Although Latinos are demographically gaining headway, without a significant investment in education or targeted interventions, their progress will be stymied. For these reasons, on college campuses, support groups such as Movimiento

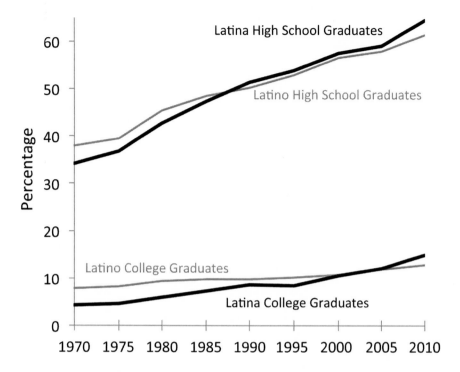

Figure 2.1. Growth in rates of high school and college graduation among Latinas (in black) and Latinos (in gray) over the last forty years. *Source: U.S. Census Bureau, 2012, Table 230.*

Estudiantil Chicano de Aztlan (MEChA), Society for Hispanic Engineers (SHPE), and Latin American Student Association (among others) provide a welcoming professional and social network for students who need support or feel marginalized on campus as a result of their minority status.

Based on quantitative measures alone, among all underrepresented minorities, Latinos are poised to have the greatest impact on the field of engineering. Latinos are currently America's largest minority population and are on the demographic fast track. As of July 2009, they comprise 16% of the total U.S. population and on average, Latinos are younger than Whites and all racial minorities (U.S. Census Bureau, 2010). These demographics suggest the potential to create a diversified workforce in engineering with Latinos helping to close the gap. As seen in Figure 2.2, Latinos are concentrated in certain states (U.S Census Bureau, Ethnicity and Ancestry Branch, Population Division, 2006). This concentration suggests that targeted interventions to attract Latinos into engineering would be most effective if they were regionally specific, and if they were specialized based on ethnic subgroup.

Nearly two-thirds of Latinos, or more than 26 million, live in California, Texas, Florida, and New York (U.S. Census Bureau, 2007).

Given that the vast majority of engineering students are White, recruiting more Latinos and Latinas would diversify and broaden participation in engineering, a strategy long overdue and critically important. "Engineering, in particular, has largely ignored the trends and failed to acknowledge that diversity drives innovation and that its absence imperils our designs, our products and our creativity" (Slaughter & McPhail, 2007). Because of the shortage of engineers and the value of a variety of life experiences for enhancing innovation, leaders are asserting the need for greater diversity in engineering education and inviting Latinos and Latinas to the table.

Gándara and Maxwell-Jolly note that research on minority programs for STEM students is lacking "a discourse of excellence" (1999). This observation is relevant beyond the research on minority programs—success in all forms is less studied. Most research focuses on why underrepresented minorities, and women of all ethnic groups, are missing from undergraduate engineering programs. Less research critically examines the social conditions that enable these groups to persist in engineering.

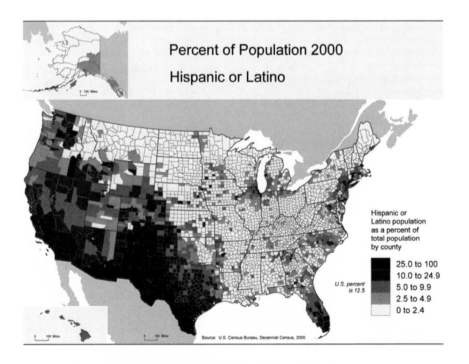

Figure 2.2. Geographic distribution of Latino population in the U.S. *Source: U.S. Census Bureau, Ethnicity and Ancestry Branch, Population Division, 2006.*

Our collaborative research has discovered that Latinas are a unique pocket of potential in the landscape of engineering education (Camacho & Lord, 2013). Latina women who matriculate into engineering do particularly well, and their rates of retention are high. The main obstacle for Latinas is that few make it through the portal into undergraduate engineering. Our society is failing to recruit Latina women into the field. The problem is a complex one. In Chapter 3, we examine Latinas who choose engineering and follow their pathways into engineering subdisciplines. Latinas are more drawn into particular engineering subdisciplines over others. This data will be useful for leaders seeking to understand the characteristics and patterns of Latinas overall.

Our data set faces some limitations. Although we are able to disaggregate by gender and ethnicity to make comparisons between Latinas, Latinos, and other racial/ethnic groups, there are many other variables that would be valuable to consider. Our data set does not give us access to social class backgrounds, geographic origins, or sexual orientation. Still, because to date there has been so little research specifically focused on Latinos and Latinas in engineering education, this analysis will begin to establish a baseline for comparative data.

CONCLUSION

In this chapter, we provided an analytical framework for understanding some of the barriers for Latina women within the field of engineering education. We addressed the historical importance of engineering innovations in the last century. We reviewed the pleas from engineering leaders indicating the need for more participation in engineering. Leaders term our failure to diversify engineering a "crisis" and suggest that U.S. prosperity and innovative potential rests on our ability to recruit and produce new engineers from diverse pools. Data from the Bureau of Labor Statistics indicates that there is a need for engineers to continue to serve clients and develop products within the United States. Engineering leaders recognize problems associated with the cultural climate of engineering, and their assertions have increasingly been responded to by federal policies and resources. Given the growth of the Latino community in the United States, based on demographics alone the potential to recruit exists. Nonetheless, structurally many barriers that correlate with poverty continue to pose challenges to this effort.

Today, the technological platforms that enabled the ubiquity of cars and mobile phones continue to influence the contours of our social environments. It is clear that the field of engineering plays a pivotal role relating technology and society. It is also clear that we need a wide range of perspectives and creative minds from all upbringings to engineer our future and to breach the borderlands of engineering.

Chapter Three

Debunking the Myths

Trajectories of Latinas in Engineering

Given U.S. Latino population increases, what is the trajectory of Latino participation in engineering education? While popular ideas about retention in science, technology, engineering, and math (STEM), suggest that women and minorities are at the greatest risk for dropping out or switching majors, recent data show that Latinos and Latinas who matriculate into engineering persist at the same rates as their White counterparts. We have seen that undergraduate engineering education has very few women and minorities (see Chapter 1, Table 1.1). Latinos who persist in engineering programs surmount one of the last exclusionary and most segregated spaces remaining in academia today.

Among Latinos and Latinas the proportion of bachelor's degrees awarded in engineering in the United States has marginally increased between 1991 and the present (National Action Council for Minorities in Engineering, 2008). Of all engineering degrees earned in 2005, for example, 7.2% were awarded to Latinos and Latinas (National Science Foundation, 2008d) and increased to 8.4% in 2009 (National Science Foundation, 2009a). Figure 3.1 illustrates the number of Latinos and Latinas in engineering slowly increasing over time. Latinas have made gains in engineering, from comprising only 4% of the Latino engineering population in 1977 to 25% in 2005.

A serious issue in research on underrepresentation is the lack of data-driven studies. Lewis suggests that some of the failures of intervention work may be due to the reliance on "folk insight [rather] than on empirical evidence" (2003, p. 361) and calls for more empirical studies in this field. In this chapter, we respond to this call and closely examine quantitative data to illuminate trends among Latinos in engineering education. We begin by ex-

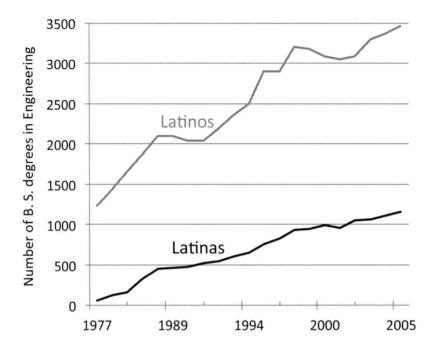

Figure 3.1.   Growth of Latinos and Latinas receiving a B.S. in engineering in the U.S. *Source: NACME 2008 p. 67 from NSF WebCASPAR database.*

amining national data for intent to major in science and engineering. Then, using a comprehensive longitudinal data set, we report six-year graduation rates disaggregated by race/ethnicity and gender to show that recruitment is a more important issue than retention. Then we focus on engineering matriculants and their six-year destinations as well as considering subdisciplines of engineering for Latinos and Latinas. Next, we consider transfer students, since the community college route is important when studying Latinos in higher education. We then describe several features of successful Latino engineers including geography and institution type. We end the chapter with some remaining challenges.

DEMOGRAPHICS OF ENGINEERING STUDENTS WITHIN STEM MAJORS

Intent to Major in Science and Engineering

Within the larger category of "science and engineering" fields (as classified by the National Science Foundation, 2008a) a gender gap between Latinos and Latinas exists. Among Latinas, the top three intended science and engineering majors were (1) social and behavioral sciences (19.9%), (2) biological and agricultural sciences (10.9%), and (3) engineering (3%). For Latino men, these were (1) engineering (18.1%), (2) social and behavioral sciences (9.3%), and (3) biological and agricultural sciences (9%). This suggests that among Latinos who are college bound, there is a strong potential for Latino men to make an impact in the field of engineering. The total female population drawn to engineering continues to be staggeringly low. Attracting Latinas to engineering will require recruitment tools specific to Latina women. See Chapter 5 for more discussion of this.

Methodology and the MIDFIELD Dataset

Although there is no national, longitudinal data for academic persistence tracking the trajectory from matriculation to graduation among Latinos, the Multiple-Institution Database for Investigating Engineering Longitudinal Development (MIDFIELD) (Long, 2008; Ohland et al., 2008) provides a unique resource for investigations of this type at 10 institutions. MIDFIELD includes records for more than 130,000 first-time-in-college (FTIC) students matriculating in engineering and over 40,000 transfer students articulating in engineering at 11 U.S. institutions, with 9 of these in the Southeastern United States. Of the U.S. engineering bachelor's degrees awarded in 2005, one-tenth were awarded by MIDFIELD institutions (ASEE, 2009). The MID-FIELD database includes 7 of the 50 largest U.S. engineering institutions by engineering enrollment (institutions in which over 20% of students major in engineering, versus the 9% national average). Race and ethnic categories are student-selected from institutional records. Results from the study of the MIDFIELD database are expected to generalize to the same type of institutions, large public universities with above average enrollment of engineering students, and therefore are relevant to institutions producing most engineering graduates nationally (ASEE, 2009). Since this data set includes whole population data, statistical inference is unnecessary—all reported differences are accurate for the institutions and subpopulations studied.

Of the total MIDFIELD population, this analysis focuses on the over 84,500 FTIC students and over 27,500 transfer students who have sufficient data to calculate six-year graduation rates during the period from 1987 to 2010. In this chapter, graduation is defined as having graduated by the sixth year from matriculation, following a standard of reporting by the Integrated Postsecondary Education Data System (IPEDS) (U.S. Department of Education, 2007).

The MIDFIELD data set allows for the examination of longitudinal trends over time; however, the former trajectory of transfer students (prior to entering a MIDFIELD institution) is unavailable. MIDFIELD permits analysis of transfer students once they enter a MIDFIELD institution and no information is available about a student's previous major. A student's progress is measured from a curricular progression standpoint to estimate how long they took to graduate. For example, if a transfer student comes in with sufficient credits to begin taking junior-level courses and finishes in three years at the MID-FIELD institution, the student would be considered to have an effective five-year time to graduation.

Note that this data set permits calculation of true graduation rates following the same students from matriculation to graduation. Such calculations are not possible with other data sets such as that of NSF that provide enrollment and graduation data for given years but provide no way to track individual students.

Recruitment, Not Retention, Is the Challenge for Latino Engineers

Using a smaller data set, we previously found that Latinos and Latinas who enter engineering education persist (i.e., do not switch majors or drop out) at numbers comparable to Whites. Of all Latinos who matriculate in engineering, 51.4% of the women and 54.6% of the men remain in engineering at the eighth semester (Lord et al., 2009, p. 178). Similarly, of Latinos who matriculated in engineering in this data set, 55.2% of the women and 52.9% of the men graduate in engineering within six years (Ohland et al., 2011). This exceeds the overall six-year graduation rate of 46.9% reported for FTIC Latinos in all majors at public four-year institutions in the United States by College Board College Completion Agenda: Latino Edition (Lee et al., 2011).

Here we include the larger MIDFIELD data set. Table 3.1 shows the number and percentage of matriculants who graduate in six years in engineering, social sciences, and science and math, which includes biological sciences, physical science, and math. Note that engineering has the highest six-year graduation rate for all race-gender combinations. Latino men and women have the highest graduation rates in engineering. Latinas graduate at slightly higher rates in social sciences than in science and math. Latinos graduate at the same rates in science and math, and social sciences. In terms of numbers, consistent with the national data, Latinos prefer engineering while Latinas prefer science and math. Although the numbers of Latinas enrolling in engineering are quite low, of those who do matriculate in engineering, the data show no significant gender gap in persistence between Latino men and women. Both men and women have the same likelihood of graduating (within 2%).

Table 3.1. Number and percentage of matriculants who graduate in six years in engineering, science and math, and social sciences.

		Engineering matriculants		Science and math matriculants		Social sciences matriculants	
		N	% of matriculants graduating in 6 years	N	% of matriculants graduating in 6 years	N	% of matriculants graduating in 6 years
Asian	Female	999	57%	2129	40%	373	31%
Asian	Male	3799	55%	2372	40%	273	29%
Black	Female	3404	45%	6371	34%	3444	39%
Black	Male	5617	38%	3629	27%	2123	31%
Latino	Female	494	47%	1649	32%	659	35%
Latino	Male	1860	45%	1436	29%	479	29%
Native American	Female	84	40%	188	32%	94	41%
Native American	Male	270	37%	166	34%	50	28%
White	Female	12713	50%	30879	39%	15441	43%
White	Male	52501	49%	29989	38%	8683	34%
Total		81741	48%	78808	37%	31619	39%

Source: MIDFIELD, FTIC, 1988–1998 matriculants.

Although common misconceptions might suggest that retention in engineering is the largest obstacle, our data show that this is not the case. Engineering is not a "weed-out" major; a landmark study confirmed what is shown in Table 3.1 and showed that engineering matriculants persist more than any other major (Ohland et al., 2008). High persistence for Latinos in engineering may be a quality unique to engineering. That is, students who are drawn toward matriculation in the field of engineering may have a higher predilection toward successful persistence. Espinosa (2009) also found that engineers had high persistence among STEM majors. She conducted a quantitative study of women in STEM using a national data set of surveys at the first and fourth year of their college careers in 2004 and 2008, respectively. She posited that strong performance in engineering is linked to the academic profiles of students:

> First, women who intended to major in engineering had both more math preparation in high school . . . and have likely fine-tuned their career ambitions at a higher level than other STEM students. Of all the STEM majors, engineering is one of the most elusive fields for secondary school students given its absence in the curriculum, with the exception perhaps of students attending math and science magnet schools, and lack of understanding of what it is that engineers do. More stringent admissions policies (especially at schools where engineering majors are impacted) given the math and physics course work required of engineering majors means that students are in the top percentile of the incoming class as it concerns academic scientific ability. (Espinosa, 2009, pp. 143–144)

Ohland et al. (2008) found that engineering majors were remarkably similar to other undergraduate students except that "(i) over 90 percent of eighth-semester students who are studying engineering had identified engineering as their major when they matriculated to college (this is much higher than any other major) and (ii) the engineering population is disproportionately male" (p. 275). As discussed in Chapter 2, the rigidity of the engineering curriculum may be a contributing factor as to why fewer students move into engineering after matriculation. This suggests that students must know they want to be engineers as soon as they enter college. Thus, the specific problem in engineering for Latinos and Latinas is primarily one of recruitment not retention (Camacho & Lord, 2013).

Engineering Matriculants in MIDFIELD

For engineering matriculants in the MIDFIELD data set, Table 3.2 shows the sixth-year destinations disaggregated by race and gender. Of those not graduating in six years, the vast majority have left the database. The destination of these students is unknown, since they could have transferred to another insti-

Table 3.2. Six-year destinations of engineering matriculants by race/ethnicity and gender.

			% of engineering matriculants		
		Engineering matriculants	Graduating in 6 years in engineering	Graduating in 6 years in any major	Not graduating in 6 years
Asian	Female	999	57%	77%	23%
Asian	Male	3799	57%	68%	32%
Black	Female	3404	46%	60%	40%
Black	Male	5617	38%	50%	50%
Latino	Female	494	50%	68%	32%
Latino	Male	1860	48%	62%	38%
Native American	Female	84	43%	57%	43%
Native American	Male	270	39%	50%	50%
White	Female	12713	54%	74%	26%
White	Male	52501	53%	67%	33%
Total		81741	48%	67%	33%

Source: MIDFIELD, FTIC, 1988–1998 matriculants.

tution, dropped out of college altogether, or be taking a break. Note that for all race/ethnicities, women are more likely than men to graduate and more than half of the engineering matriculants graduate from college in six years. Engineering is the most likely sixth-year destination for most engineering matriculants including Latino men and women. Not graduating is the most likely destination for Black and Native American men, and graduating in engineering and not graduating are very close for Native American women. This is symptomatic of larger structural issues (Lord et al., 2009).

LATINOS AND LATINAS WHO PERSIST IN ENGINEERING EDUCATION

Latinos/as in MIDFIELD

What happens to Latino men and women who matriculate in engineering? Table 3.3 shows the six-year destinations for Latino/a engineering matriculants in MIDFIELD. The order of destinations does not vary by gender. By far the most likely destination is to graduate in engineering for men and women. The second mostly likely destination is to leave the database. Science/math is the next most popular major, and business is the third. Of the

Table 3.3. Six-year destinations of 494 Latina and 1,860 Latino engineering matriculants.

6th year destination	Latinas		Latinos	
	N	%	N	%
Graduate in engineering	233	47%	841	45%
Leave database*	130	26%	636	34%
Graduate in science & math	34	7%	88	5%
Did not graduate in 6 years (still working on degree)	28	6%	77	4%
Graduate in business	27	5%	68	4%
Graduate in other majors	20	4%	38	2%
Graduate in social sciences	12	2%	48	3%
Graduate in arts & humanities	8	2%	22	1%
Graduate in technology	2	0%	42	2%

Source: MIDFIELD, FTIC, 1988–1998 matriculants.
*Leaving the database means that their destination is unknown. This could include transferring to another institution, dropping out of school, or taking a long break from college.

Latino/a students who did not graduate in six years, 13 women and 47 men graduated in engineering in more than six years. Four women and 14 men in the data set never graduated. The remainder graduated in more than six years in other majors.

The research of Seymour and Hewett (1997) showed that men and women migrate into and out of engineering for different reasons. The power of the MIDFIELD data set allows us to see the exact destinations with great specificity. Although the numbers here are small, overall the numbers of Latinos/as in higher education nationally continue to be small. Therefore this unique database provides us with one powerful view into their destinations. Most significant is the profound percentage of Latinos and Latinas that are successful in graduating in engineering. As seen in Table 3.1, these rates are significantly greater than those in other majors.

Engineering Subdisciplines

Among all Latinos who do enter undergraduate engineering, analysis of the variability among subdisciplines merits consideration. The degree-earning patterns among Latinos in engineering are consistent with those of students of all ethnic groups. The top three overall choices of Latinos match those of Blacks and overlap with those of Whites and Native Americans. There is considerable variation, however, by gender. Figure 3.2 shows the distribution of engineering bachelor's degrees awarded to Latinos in the United States 2000–2008 (NSF, 2008b; NSF, 2008c) disaggregated by gender. Note that the top three subdisciplines for Latino men are electrical, mechanical, and civil engineering with about 60% choosing electrical or mechanical. However, Latinas tend to be more evenly distributed throughout the engineering subdisciplines with electrical and mechanical accounting for only 36% of Latina engineers. The top two subdisciplines for Latinas are (1) civil and (2) electrical, with mechanical, industrial, and chemical each tied for third with about 14% each. According to the Bureau of Labor Statistics (2007), engineering employment opportunities are expected to grow from about 1.5 million engineering jobs in the United States in 2006 to a projected 1.7 million jobs by 2016. Given the large pool of aging, currently employed engineers that are projected to retire, and the decreasing number of new "traditional" (White male) engineering students, such projected employment opportunities will be met with a deficit of engineers unless efforts are made to diversify the profession. The highest growth is expected in the fields of biomedical, civil, and industrial engineering. This holds particular promise for Latinas because they are more attracted to industrial and civil engineering than men.

Researchers have begun to explore the reasons why women prefer some engineering subdisciplines over others. Early socialization, influence of parents and teachers, academic preparation and success, work experience, and networks have been cited as important factors (Margolis & Fisher, 2002; Tillberg & Cahoon, 2005). The most significant work to date has been done with industrial engineering. Researchers have described industrial engineering as occupying a "borderland" in engineering with overlap in business and significant emphasis on human beings and their interaction with technology (Foor & Walden, 2009). Industrial engineering has been shown to be the only engineering major that gains women and men from the third semester through six-year graduation and among all race-gender combinations (except Black men) (Brawner et al., 2012). Women undergraduates majoring in industrial engineering described a variety of reasons why they were drawn to industrial engineering. These include warmth, flexibility, a sense it is more feminine, and career opportunities (Brawner et al., 2012). Very little research to date specifically examines reasons why women choose civil engineering, an important field commonly offered at engineering schools. Some possibilities for the attractiveness of civil engineering for women include good job opportunities (Baryeh, Squire, & Mogotsi, 2001), an attraction to building things, and interest in working for the government or as a consultant. Civil engineering, whose name comes from its civilian rather than nonmilitary focus, involves designing and building items such as roads, bridges, and buildings. Because this involves understanding the surrounding environment, environmental engineering is considered a subdiscipline of civil. Environmental engineering has been labeled as a more "feminine" type of engineering (Zengin-Arslan, 2002). This may be because of perceptions that "environmental" is linked to conservation, "green technology," or helping the environment. Since "feminine" is socially constructed to include nurturing, perhaps environmental engineering is seen as a material way to transform and improve the physical environment.

Some research suggests that women prefer majors with a clear benefit to society; thus researchers advocate providing meaningful contexts for problem solving and applications to help attract women (Davis & Rosser, 1996). However, this essentialist notion that women are primarily attracted to engineering fields that "help people" is not substantiated in other studies (Hartman, Hartman, & Kadlowec, 2007; Kilgore, Shepard, Atman, & Chachra, 2011). Hartman, Hartman, and Kadlowec (2007) surveyed first-year female engineering students in mechanical and electrical engineering (not as popular with women and perceived as less "helping") and compared them with those in chemical and civil/environmental engineering (more popular with women and seen as more "helping"). They found that background differences, differences in general academic and math/science self-confidence, attributions of success, and expectations about the engineering degree did not account for the differences in proportions of women in the different engineering majors.

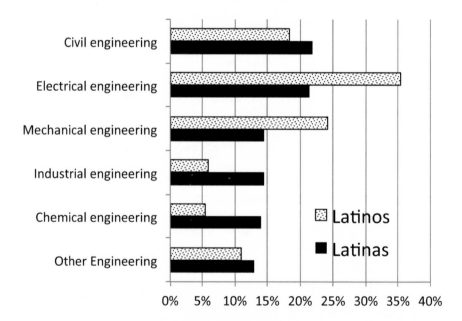

Figure 3.2.   Distribution of bachelor's degrees of Latinos and Latinas in engineering subdisciplines for 2000–2008, N for Latinos is 30,902 and for Latinas is 9,917. *Source: NSF Division of Science Resource Statistics, Tables 5-4 and 5-5.*

No statistically significant differences were found between women and men in all majors regarding their expectation that their engineering degree would help them make an important contribution to society. The researchers did find differences in the reported engineering self-confidence of women entering the different majors. In the Academic Pathways Survey (APS), a large national survey with over 4,000 respondents from 21 institutions, researchers found that men and women had similar motivations for studying engineering with intrinsic motivation being highest for all students (Kilgore et al., 2011). Motivation to study engineering for social good was a close second with men and women citing this motivation in virtually equal rates (74.6% for women and 74.1% for men). More research is needed on the persistence of women in different engineering subdisciplines, especially that disaggregated by race and gender, such as that by Lord, Layton, and Ohland for electrical and computer engineering (2011). Further qualitative analysis is necessary to understand the reasons why students choose specific engineering subdisciplines and more research is certainly needed to understand how Latinas interpret the possibilities for success in the disciplines.

TRANSFER STUDENTS

Although only a small number of first-time-in-college (FTIC) matriculants or internal transfers migrate into engineering from other majors, the pool of external transfer students into engineering is substantial. Often originating at community colleges, transfer students provide a potential source of many engineers and a more diverse population of engineers (Brainard, 2008). This potential is particularly true for Latinos in our data set where 40% of the Latino students who are ever engineers are transfers, higher than the 30% for White students. For comparison, in national data from the U.S. Department of Education, in fall 2007, 34% of White and 40% of Black college students were in community colleges while 51% of Latino college students were in community colleges (National Center for Education Statistics, 2008).

Examining the trajectories of transfer students is methodologically difficult and there are mixed results reported in the literature. Some studies show that transfer students are less likely to achieve academically than students who matriculate in four-year institutions (Pascarella & Terenzini, 2005) while others show that transfer students, after initial "transfer shock" or decrease in GPA upon transfer (Hills, 1965), may actually do as well or better than "native" students (Glass & Harrington, 2002). Brainard asserts that engineering students who transfer from two-year to four-year institutions do well, earning better grades and graduating at slightly higher rates than native students (2008). The primary challenge to drawing from the transfer population, however, is that few students actually transfer with estimates at about one-third (Brainard, 2008). Transfer students in engineering are the focus of a 2005 National Academies Press report entitled "The Community College Pathway to Engineering Careers" (Mattis & Sislen, 2005). Engineering transfer students may encounter unique challenges including rigid prerequisites (Kerr, 2006), inadequate preparation for rigorous upper division courses (Graham, 2007), and more intense transfer shock than students in nontechnical majors (Cejda, Kaylor, & Rewey, 1998), which negatively affect their self-efficacy related to academic milestones such as GPA (Concannon & Barrow, 2009). Concannon and Barrow (2009) examined the separate impacts of race, gender, and transfer status for engineering students. They found no significant differences in overall self-efficacy by gender, transfer status, or race for Hispanics; however, they had only 12 Hispanic students participate in their survey. More discussion of community colleges, many of which have large populations of Latino students, is found in Chapter 5.

Table 3.4 shows the number and six-year destinations for engineering transfer students by race/ethnicity and gender from MIDFIELD. Note that all engineering transfer students are highly likely to graduate in engineering and to graduate from college. The high graduation rates of engineering transfer

Table 3.4. Number and six-year destinations of engineering transfer students by race/ethnicity and gender.

			% of engineering transfer students		
		First major engineering N	Graduating in 6 years in engineering	Graduating in 6 years in any major	Not graduating in 6 years
Asian	Female	397	62%	74%	26%
Asian	Male	1687	63%	71%	29%
Black	Female	1004	55%	63%	37%
Black	Male	1834	49%	56%	44%
Latino	Female	191	72%	82%	18%
Latino	Male	848	63%	70%	30%
Native Am	Female	26	46%	58%	42%
Native Am	Male	136	53%	59%	41%
White	Female	3328	55%	69%	31%
White	Male	16159	57%	66%	34%
Total	Female	397	62%	74%	26%
Total	Male	1687	63%	71%	29%
TOTAL		25610	57%	66%	34%

Source: MIDFIELD, 1988–1998 start years.

students may be due to these students having already successfully passed many lower-division courses. Transfer students have firsthand experience with the rigorous curriculum of the major; they have already surmounted many hoops, are more knowledgeable about the major, and thus more invested in a commitment to success.

Latino transfers in engineering are particularly successful. Latino males have graduation rates in engineering only surpassed by Asian males. They leave the database at rates comparable to Asian and White males. Latinas, are the most successful among all transfer students, having the highest six-year graduation rate in engineering, the highest rate of graduation in any major, and are the least likely to drop out of school. Only 18% of Latina engineering transfer students left the database, which means that 82% graduated! These successes may be related to what several researchers describe as the "personal agency, or internal drive," of women of color in college that contributes to their persistence (Espinosa, 2009) including Latinas in information technology (Varma, 2002) and Chicana and Latina transfer students in science and math (Valenzuela, 2006). Valenzuela called this *"mi fuerza"* or "inner fire to succeed" (2006, p. 88).

SUCCESSES

Geography Matters

The American Society for Engineering Education (ASEE) conducts an annual survey of U.S. colleges and universities with engineering programs and publishes an annual report with the results. Table 3.5 shows the number of engineering bachelor's degrees awarded to Latinos/as from these ASEE reports for 2001–2002, 2007–2008, and 2009–2010 combined (Gibbons, 2002; 2008; 2010). Note that over 320 institutions across the United States were included each year. The top two schools for Latino/a engineers each year are from Puerto Rico and have many more students than the next ranking institution. Note that eleven of the top twenty (55%) institutions are designated as Hispanic Serving Institutions by the Hispanic Association of Colleges and Universities (HACU, n.d.). Many of the other institutions are large public schools in states with large Latino populations such as Texas, Florida, Georgia, and California. The only school in a state without large Latino populations is the Massachusetts Institute of Technology (MIT), which is perhaps the most prestigious and well-known engineering school in the United States.

The case of engineering programs in Puerto Rico merits close analysis. Not only do Puerto Rico schools graduate by far the most Latino engineers as seen in Table 3.5, they also have exceptionally high percentages of women. At the University of Puerto Rico–Mayguez (UPRM), 39.6% of the engineering bachelor's degrees in 2002 and 2010 were awarded to women and 35.6%

Table 3.5.   Engineering bachelor's degrees awarded to Hispanics by school.

Rank	Institution	Number
1	Univ. of Puerto Rico, Mayaguez*	1872
2	Polytechnic Univ. of Puerto Rico*	1283
3	Florida International University*	781
4	University of Texas, El Paso*	489
5	University of Florida	427
6	California State Poly. Univ., Pomona*	365
7	University of Texas, Austin	343
8	Texas A&M University	328
9	California Poly. State Univ., SLO	279
10	University of Texas, Pan American*	232
11	Arizona State University	218
12	University of Central Florida	215
13	Massachusetts Institute of Technology	212
14	Texas A&M University, Kingsville*	203
15	New Mexico State University*	193
16	University of Texas, San Antonio*	162
17	Georgia Institute of Technology	144
18	San Jose State University	131
19	California State Univ., Long Beach*	85
20	City College of the CUNY*	81

Source: ASEE Data for 2002, 2008, and 2010. 320 Schools reporting in 2002, 339 in 2008, and 344 in 2010.
* indicates Hispanic-serving institution (HSI).

in 2008 (Gibbons, 2002; 2008; 2010). These are among the highest percentages (in the top five) for women reported in the ASEE national data and include over 200 women each year, which makes this institution rank in the top six for *numbers* of women receiving engineering degrees in the United States. This campus's engineering programs are accredited by ABET, the same body that accredits engineering programs on the mainland in the United States (ABET, 2012b). This suggests that the differences in percentage of women graduates are not due to a different curriculum. Puerto Rico's unique geographic and historical context raises questions. To what extent does this critical mass draw women into the field and provide a cultural context that is more inviting and supportive to help women to graduate and succeed? Very little research has been done in this area. A notable exception is the work of

Cruz-Pol and Colom-Ustáriz (2002) who studied women undergraduates in engineering at UPRM. Their survey results from a sample of 36 Latinas revealed that the five most common reasons given by these women for the large percentage of women at UPRM were "cultural reasons, role models, encouragement by parents, motivation in high school, and encouragement by high school teachers" (p. 1). The most important factors that these women cited as contributing to their decision to study engineering were "good in Science and Math in High School, engineering viewed as empowering career, parents/relative motivation, did well in College board examination (SAT), and prestigious career" (p. 1). The authors also point out that the cost of education at UPRM is much lower than is typical on the U.S. mainland and over 80% of the students receive government financial aid so that most students do not need work while going to school. UPRM also attracts the top students from Puerto Rico and is considered quite prestigious. More research is needed to examine the conditions in Puerto Rico that result in attracting, retaining, and graduating such an exceptionally high percentage of women in engineering education.

Success of Hispanic-Serving Institutions for Latinos and Latinas in Engineering

Institution type has a significant effect on Latino graduation rates in engineering; HSIs show the most growth in graduating Latino engineers. Figure 3.3 shows the distribution of Latino (U.S. citizen and permanent resident) engineering bachelor's degree recipients by institution type (all institutions and HSIs or High Hispanic Enrollment [HHE]) from 1994 to 2008 (NSF 2008e; NSF 2009b).

Non-science and engineering (non-S&E) fields are by far the most popular for Latinos at all institutions accounting for about 70% of degree recipients overall. Sciences account for about 27% and engineering about 5%. For all institutions, there has been more than a twofold growth in degree attainment for Latinos in all fields from 1994 to 2008. Engineering has shown the least growth, at about a factor of 1.7 while non-S&E has increased by a factor of 2.2. HSIs play a critical role here. From 1994 to 2001, HSIs experienced a 36% growth in engineering degrees compared to 23% for non-HSIs (Camacho & Lord, 2011b). HSIs hold great promise for graduating future Latino engineers. Since 1994, about 40% of the engineering degrees awarded to Latinos have been at HSIs or HHEs while only 30% of science degrees were awarded at such institutions.

Several causal mechanisms may explain why HSIs and HHEs are successful with Latino engineers. The geographic location of most HSIs and HHEs near Latino communities may allow students to maintain close ties to family, home, and the larger ethnic enclave, lessening social isolation, which

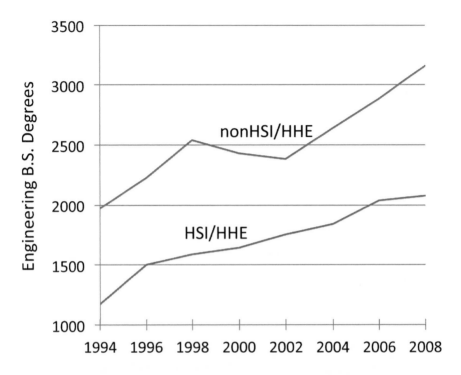

**Figure 3.3.   Growth in Latinos receiving B.S. degrees in engineering in the Unit-
ed States by institution type: HSIs play a significant role. Note that data for
1994–1999 uses HSI while 2000–2008 uses High Hispanic Enrollment (HHE).**
*Source: NSF, Division of Science Resources Statistics, special tabulations of
U.S. Department of Education, National Center for Education Statistics, Integrated Postsecondary Education Data System, Completions Survey, 1994–2009.*

they are more likely to experience at predominantly White campuses. One
cannot underestimate the comfort of being in a place where it is easy to find
familiar foods, music on radio stations, and friends of similar backgrounds.
All students face challenges when adapting to college. For Latinos at a predominantly White institution, there is the additional challenge of adapting to
a different cultural context. This additional challenge would not be as salient
at an HSI or HHE. Hurtado and Carter (1997) describe this holistic student
experience as a "sense of belonging." This sense of belonging has been found
to be important for retention of college students (Hoffman, Richmond, Morrow, & Salomone, 2002). In an exploratory study of Latino students' sense of
belonging at an HSI, Maestas, Vaquera, & Zehr (2007) found that factors that
increased Latino students' sense of belonging included participating in academic support programs, faculty interest in student development, and living
on campus. The institutional staff at HSIs and HHEs may be more adept at

recognizing and supporting the academic and cultural needs of Latino students. Finally, greater numbers of faculty and administrative role models may promote academic persistence by providing mentorship and personal advising (Laden, 2001). Examining this sense of belonging and the factors leading to success, particularly within the unique context of Latinas at HSIs, continues to be an important area of ongoing research. More research is needed focusing on specific disciplines such as engineering.

A REMAINING CHALLENGE: FACULTY DEMOGRAPHICS IN ENGINEERING AND SCIENCES

Among faculty, women continue to be severely underrepresented in the sciences and particularly in engineering as seen in Table 3.6 (Beutel & Nelson, 2005). Very few faculty members are Latinos and Latinas. In this data set, of the almost 7,000 faculty of all ethnic and racial groups in engineering, only 8% are women and only 0.2% are Latina. This highlights again the significant gender barrier that exists and remains a crisis in engineering education. Data for physical sciences is similar to engineering with 8% women and 2% Latino. Women have higher representation in the biological sciences with 20%, social sciences with 23%, and psychology with 33%. Latino men and women are only 2% of the faculty of the biological sciences and 3% for social sciences and psychology. Engineering has a higher non-White population compared to all of the sciences due to the large number of Asian faculty. All of the sciences are over 85% White.

According to the ASEE national data shown in Figure 3.4 (Gibbons, 2010; Yoder, 2011), women have made some gains in their participation in engineering faculty in the last decade rising from 8.9% in 2001 to 13.8% in 2011. Women comprised over 23% of assistant professors in 2011, which shows promise for the future although there is still a long way to go to achieve parity. As of 2011, only 8.7% of full professors and 15.8% of asso-

Table 3.6. Distribution of male and female faculty by race-ethnicity for top engineering research departments.

Engineering faculty	White	Black	Latino	Asian	All groups	Percentage
Male	4777	85	160	1246	6268	92%
Female	461	14	11	94	580	8%
Total N	5238	99	171	1340	6848	
Percentage	76%	1%	2%	20%	100%	

Source: Adapted from Beutel and Nelson, 2005.

ciate professors in engineering are women. The percentage of Asian faculty members in engineering has increased over the last decade but virtually no gains have been made for African American or Latino engineering faculty, although this ASEE report does include faculty data from UPRM and Polytechnic University of Puerto Rico. Latino faculty are distributed throughout a variety of engineering subdisciplines (Yoder, 2011). It is interesting that the data show that Latinos are attracted to more interdisciplinary fields, since the highest percentage of Latino faculty are found in interdisciplinary fields: engineering management, civil/environmental, engineering (general), and industrial/manufacturing. These are not, however, the fields that attract the largest numbers of non-Latino engineering faculty.

Certainly the low numbers of women and Latino/a faculty are correlated with the low numbers of women and Latinos/as receiving bachelor's degrees in engineering. Because engineering is a career where a good job can be obtained with a bachelor's degree, many students do not pursue graduate school and thus are not able to join academic faculty ranks. Many programs are focused on increasing diversity in STEM fields at all levels (Malcolm, Chubin, & Jesse, 2004). To enlarge and diversify the pool for academia,

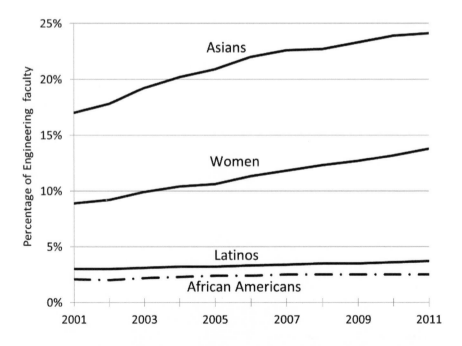

Figure 3.4. Demographics of engineering faculty from 2001 to 2011: Growth for women and Asians but not for Latinos and African Americans. *Source: ASEE 2010 and 2011 Profiles of Engineering and Engineering Technology Colleges.*

there are efforts to encourage more underrepresented students to go to graduate school (McNair, 2012), support them in graduate programs (Davis et al., 2006; Purdy et al., 2007; Purdy et al., 2008) and to study the experiences of these students (Chapa & De la Rosa, 2006; Gándara, 2006; Millet & Nettles, 2006). The low numbers of Latino and Latina faculty members compound the pipeline issues. Sonnert, Fox, and Adkins (2007) specifically found higher persistence of women students in STEM majors with higher representation of women faculty. As Espinosa says,

> Faculty diversity in STEM is of principal importance given the literature on the educational benefits of faculty-student mentorship for women and minority students in undergraduate STEM education (Alfred, Atkins, Lopez, Chavez, Avila, & Paolini, 2005; Maton, Hrabowski, & Schmitt, 2000; National Research Council, 2006; Santovec, 1999; Seymour & Hewitt, 1997). The lack of women of color in academic STEM positions means lost opportunity for young women in need of role models and mentors that understand the unique space women of color occupy in STEM majors and departments. Finally, all students reap educational rewards when learning alongside a diverse peer group (Antonio, 2001; Antonio, Chang, Hakuta, Kenny, Levin, & Milem, 2004; Chang, 2001, 2003; Chang, Denson, Saenz, & Misa, 2006; Gurin, Dey, Hurtado, & Gurin, 2002; Hurtado, 2001), an important element of STEM persistence and graduate degree ambitions for women (Tsui, 1995), with additional impact on overall sense of belonging for minority students (Maestas, Vaquera, & Zehr, 2007; Locks, Hurtado, Bowman, & Oseguera, 2008). (2009, p. 7)

Discrimination continues to play a role in the diversification of faculty. Sue Rosser documents this through powerful stories of successful women in science and engineering (2012). Researchers have begun to investigate faculty-hiring processes to identify and suggest strategies to minimize implicit and explicit biases against women and people of color (Bilimoria & Buch, 2010; Smith, Turner, Osei-Kofi, & Richards, 2004; Turner, Gonzalez, & Wood, 2008). The National Science Foundation ADVANCE program specifically funds efforts in this area with the goal to transform academic environments to promote the success of women faculty in STEM.

NEXT STEPS

The quantitative analysis in this chapter reveals that Latinos/as who choose to major in engineering are successful. To understand more about their experiences and why they are successful, we need to hear the voices of Latinas majoring in engineering. Such qualitative analysis is the topic of Chapter 4. Recruiting Latinas into engineering remains a challenge. Given that Latinas who transfer into engineering are particularly successful, this appears to be a promising pathway for Latinos/as into engineering. Many Latinos enroll in community colleges, including two-year HSIs, before transferring to four-year institutions (Laden, 2001). This is considered in more detail in Chapter 5 along with other strategies for recruiting Latinas into engineering.

Chapter Four

Voices of Latinas in Engineering

How do Latina women experience the climate of engineering undergraduate education? As reviewed in Chapter 3, from a quantitative perspective, inequities for women and underrepresented minorities in engineering education are stark. Within the male-dominated culture of engineering, both overt and subtle practices serve to construct the experiences of women undergraduates. Women continue to experience the climate in engineering differently from men (Camacho, Lord, Brawner, & Ohland, 2010; Lattuca, Terenzini, & Volkwein, 2006). We used a case study approach to understand the experiences of Latina engineers enrolled in engineering programs at a large public institution in the southeastern United States. The objective of the case study approach is to triangulate the quantitative data on persistence of Latina engineers with qualitative data drawn from focus group research. This approach allowed us to intensively examine the experiences of Latinas within one particular engineering education climate. More than twenty-five years ago, Ortiz found that the successful Latinas in college "did not become assimilated into the university milieu, but they do perform well" (1986, p. 137). Compared with Ortiz's study, the Latinas in our study reported struggling with isolation, although they do not report being as isolated as their earlier counterparts, who were often the only Latina in any of their classes, particularly in math and science. Our qualitative research is part of a larger study in which we also conducted focus groups with women majoring in various engineering subdisciplines (Brawner, Lord, & Ohland, 2011; Brawner, Camacho, Lord, Long, & Ohland, 2012) and separately with women engineering students who self-identify as Asian American, Latina, Black, and White (Camacho & Lord, 2011a).

In this chapter, we draw on our qualitative research among Latina students to examine their experiences of the academic and social aspects of the climate of undergraduate engineering education. Qualitative research, incorporating the rich, detailed perspectives through the women's voices, adds value to our understanding of the quantitative reality of engineering as a segregated space in academia. Our findings suggest that Latinas in engineering redefine ideas of success, which paradoxically, focus on learning how to fail. For example, Latinas in focus groups described their adjustment to forced curves; engineering educational assessment often relies on such "curved grades" for weeding out majors. They also described how they overcame inhibitions of failure, and effectively learned not to be psychically devastated by receiving a low grade, given they had been high achievers in high school. They also discuss how they cope socially, in the face of some adversity, in order to persist in undergraduate engineering courses. We use a microaggressions framework to organize our findings.

MICROAGGRESSIONS IN ENGINEERING EDUCATION

Several ethnic studies scholars have demonstrated how "microaggressions" in academic settings against Blacks and Latinos can have a profound impact on perceptions of inclusion, as can marginal status in terms of gender and sexual orientation (Solórzano, Ceja, & Yosso, 2000; Sue, 2010; Yosso, Smith, Ceja, & Solórzano, 2009). Racialized microaggressions are "brief and commonplace daily verbal, behavioral, or environmental indignities, whether intentional or unintentional, that communicate hostile, derogatory, or negative racial slights and insults toward people of color" (Sue et al., 2007, p. 271). Researchers suggest that subtle and covert racist and sexist acts serve as microaggressions and occur frequently in the lives of subordinated groups (Pierce, 1970). Microaggressions can negatively affect an individual's psyche and can take an emotional toll among recipients (Pierce, 1995; Solórzano, Ceja, & Yosso, 2000; Yosso, Smith, Ceja, & Solórzano, 2009). According to the theory of microaggressions, interpersonal comments and interactions that are perceived as offensive by a recipient are often not intended as such (Sue, 2010). Researchers have found instances of microaggressions in the experiences of women of color in STEM classrooms including feeling unwelcome, unsupported, or invisible (Espinosa, 2009; Ortiz, 1986; Sosnowski, 2002, cited in Espinosa, 2009; Varma, Prasad, & Kapur, 2006, cited in Espinosa, 2009).

Although there is somewhat of a shared experience among undergraduate engineering women, microaggressions are processed differently depending on race/ethnicity. Some undergraduates enter college and are immediately exposed to stereotypes that precede them. For example, Asian students are often stereotyped as the "model minority," that is, as students destined for academic success regardless of social class background or gender (Lee,

2009). The model minority idea, however, is problematic and has been more recently dubbed the "model minority myth" (Chou & Feagin, 2008; Trytten, Lowe, & Walden, 2012) because it fails to take into account diverse sociohistorical characteristics of Asian communities, which we referred to in Chapter 2. Black and Latino students, by contrast, are frequently dubbed by their peers as "affirmative action babies"—they are perceived as students who were admitted to the university based on their race as the primary criterion, rather than on academic merit. For example, Varma (2002, cited in Espinosa, 2009) found that Latina undergraduate women in information technology felt that their style made them appear less intelligent than other women; they also often felt that professors viewed them as affirmative action tokens.

Microaggressions can be experienced by women in engineering in many forms. They can be experienced at the institutional level (such as through biases in the curriculum, structure, and type of assignments, and even in accepted canons of the knowledge base), at the interpersonal level (in the form of snubs, dismissive gestures, or seemingly innocent comments that are perceived as hurtful, inappropriate, or insulting), and finally as jokes and humor that subtly deride women's place in engineering. Note that these are not three discrete categories; experiences overlap among them.

For undergraduate engineering students, the traditional culture of engineering education breeds some animosity among students, given competitive modes of assessment. How do women in engineering education experience student segmentation, such as through curved grading? Curved grading can serve as a mechanism of power that reinforces stratification (Fines, 1997). Do women internalize feelings of failure? How do they adapt to the spirit of engineering, one that routinely emphasizes the value of "hard" and rigorous tradition of education (Stevens, Amos, Garrison, & Jocuns, 2007). In terms of collaboration and team projects, women are sometimes made to assume a traditionally feminine role (such as team secretary) or, alternatively, are simply ignored as if they were invisible.

CASE STUDY OF LATINA ENGINEERS: QUALITATIVE METHODS

The case study approach of Latinas in engineering allows for intensive analysis (Stake, 1995; Yin, 2008). We focused on one large public university with a fairly diverse student body so that we could identify sufficient numbers of women of color in engineering. The school is technically focused with a considerable amount of prestige associated with its engineering programs. As a result, student perceptions indicate that other majors are devalued. Similarly, students who choose this university are interested in technical majors. As a result there are not many options for switching majors, though some students are drawn to business/management.

For the data collection, we used focus groups given that this methodology provides rich descriptions of the participants' shared experiences. Focus groups are particularly helpful for gathering information from groups that are often marginalized and might be put off by or unresponsive to direct questioning in interviews. Focus group methods offer "a unique opportunity to study individuals in their social contexts, by generating high-quality interactive data, by contributing to the social construction of meaning, and by accessing women's shared, and often ignored, stocks of knowledge" (Madriz, 2003, p. 383). Having a Latina interviewer, with expertise in ethnic studies and sociology, enhanced our ability to get these engineering students to talk about typically difficult issues surrounding race and gender. Students majoring in STEM fields typically do not have experience talking about such issues and may initially deny experiencing any racism or sexism (Cohoon, Nable, & Boucher, 2011).

There are three limitations to our approach. First, our sample was limited to "persisters" (students who matriculated in engineering and continue in the major)—students who switched majors, transferred, or dropped out of engineering are excluded from this pool of participants. Another limitation is one commonly faced by qualitative researchers who study race/ethnicity: there is considerable variability within each group, based on social class, parentage, languages spoken and regional difference, among others. Finally, our sample allowed for the inclusion of various engineering majors, and did not attempt to control for subdiscipline (i.e., electrical engineering vs. chemical engineering); the data set is too small to examine this.

We held focus groups with a total of 21 women engineering undergraduates in February 2010. Students were invited to participate in the groups by a person on campus who had access to lists of women in engineering. Students ranged in age from 19 to 26 and were sophomores through seniors. Participants volunteered to participate based on their availability, interest in the subject, and probably because of the honorarium. Each student received $20 for her participation. All focus groups were recorded and transcribed verbatim. We removed most fillers (i.e., "um" and "like") in the data reporting.

The desired number of students for each group was 8 to 10 since larger groups are too difficult to moderate. A large sample size was not part of the objectives of this portion of the study. With our case study approach the goal was to describe, understand, and explain social characteristics of Latinas using their own words and interpretations of their subjective roles in engineering. An additional objective was to triangulate these findings with our quantitative data to broaden our analysis. The sample size is too small for generalizability, but the objectives of the approach were achieved (see Yin, 2008). The Asian group had 6 students, the Latina group had 5, and the White group had 10. All of the Asian women, 9 of the White women (90%), and 2 of the Latinas (40%) reported having family members who were engineers. In this chapter, we closely examine the data from the focus group with Latina engineers, and in some cases offer comparison with other groups.

CASE STUDY OF LATINA ENGINEERS: FINDINGS AND ANALYSIS

We found that students easily discussed and shared their experiences in terms of their roles as undergraduate women in engineering. They shared diverse reasons for wanting to study engineering. We asked them general questions about why they chose to major in engineering, the campus climate, and their support mechanisms. We also asked open-ended questions, such as "What advice would you give to incoming students like you in engineering?" and "Describe the biggest obstacle you overcame in this engineering program and how you overcame it." In addition to themes associated with climate in engineering, they also discussed their perseverance in the engineering major and their gendered experiences as women in a male-dominated space. Here, we organize our findings using these themes.

Reasons for Studying Engineering among Latinas

Given the low numbers of women in engineering, researchers have long been interested in the factors that draw women in. Motives for wanting to pursue a major in engineering range from perceived skill in math and science to parental or familial inspiration, to a desire to contribute uniquely to society. When asked why they decided to study engineering, the theme of having a family member role model emerged most frequently. One Latina respondent said, "My cousin is an electrical engineer in Colombia, and when I was little I would go to my grandmother's house where he lived over the summer. And I'd just see him working on the little circuit boards that they have, and it all seemed really interesting to me so that's kind of how I got into it." Another Latina was inspired by her parents, who were both engineers:

> My dad's electrical and my mom's chemical. And my dad's really quiet—he doesn't bring work home, but my mom . . . she likes bringing work home and is always talking about it. So as a little girl I always heard about it. And then when I got older and I did chemistry and math and all those sciences. [I] started liking it, so I guess it was [that] or because of my mom.

Given that there are so many more men who are engineers, it is not uncommon that a male role model inspired these students. In the absence of engineering family members, Latina students still described the important role of parental guidance: "My dad, he's not a civil engineer or anything, but whenever we go anywhere and drive anywhere, if he sees a bridge or a construction project, he stops the car and makes us all get out and talks about it. So that kind of sparked my interest."

Other Latinas described a long-time affinity toward math and science: "I always liked math and science, and whenever I would tell people that, they'd be like, oh, you should be an engineer. And when I did more research into it I realized that [I] wanted more involvement with practical applications rather than really the science behind it. That's why I chose engineering versus . . . a science major." Another echoed this sentiment: "I've always liked math and science more . . . history has never appealed to me [or] the social sciences. . . . They're just not my thing." Wanting to help society was also mentioned: "After I heard that in [Latin America] construction is really poor, I always thought that I would, I wanted to, help. I wanted to contribute to study civil engineering and make things better." Although this student was born in the United States, she possesses a transnational affinity to her parental homeland, and a desire to improve it materially. Her belief is that working in engineering can make a difference abroad.

Latina engineering students also experience detractors, people who second-guess their commitment to pursuing engineering. One Latina expressed it like this:

> A couple of people told me, "Why do you want to do some engineering? That's mainly for guys. And you know, you could do architecture. That would fit more with you." And I was like, yeah, probably, but I really like some engineering, and I mean, even though guys do that, I think I'm capable of doing it too, because nowadays, we, women and men, do the same thing. . . . And then after that, when I got [to this university], nothing may change my decision. [But] I didn't [understand] the experience until I got here and I actually saw it, because you see it's so many guys.

When asked how they respond to this context, Latinas expressed concerns but also mentioned how they persevere by trying to ignore the context or by adopting the same competitive attitude of those around them:

> I think that that's just a little scarier, because you always assume guys are smarter in math and science, so that kinda, I guess, makes it just a little scary to go into the field. I mean I just didn't put that in mind as much.

Another said,

> I feel like it sort of sparked a competitive drive in me. My mom, she's Latina. She's Latina and she's an engineer. And, you know I guess it's more noticeable in her because she has a very thick accent, so she always struggled. And I was always like, "Hold on. No, no, no, no. No, no, no. I—I'm gonna do better [chuckles]. I'm gonna do better." So, yeah, I guess it was that competitive edge almost.

Echoing this respondent another added, "I think it was just having that drive of yes, it's a male-dominated field. But it's something that I want to do. It's something that I'm passionate about. And I mean, I don't know everybody else's high schools, but . . . in all the classes it was primarily White males. And, it was just something I was accustomed to, and I'd already dealt with it in the past and, you know, was gonna deal with it again."

These themes resonate with other qualitative research on women in engineering. Frequently women engineers get a start on their careers with the inspiration of a family member who works in engineering. Because of the lack of engineering classes at the high school level, it is often a predilection toward math and science at the high school level that leads them toward an engineering major. For example, in their study of Latina engineering majors at the University of Puerto Rico–Mayaguez, Cruz-Pol and Colom-Ustáriz (2002) found that the most commonly cited reason for deciding to study engineering was being "good in science and math in high school." Their experiences leading up to the major in some ways prepare them for the unique experience of being a double minority in the engineering college classroom.

Interpersonal Microaggressions

Many students described their gender-experiences in terms of their perceived sense of belonging at the specific institution. For example, students described with mixed emotion the sense that outsiders insinuate they are not a good fit for engineering. For example, women of all ethnic groups, with some subtle differences, commented that outsiders express some shock or surprise that they, as women, are studying engineering. One Latina student, for example said, "When you tell them you're an engineering major, then they act even more surprised. So I think that that's kind of an assumption just because you're a girl." Similarly, an Asian woman said, "If I tell people outside of engineering, outside of [this institution], that I'm an engineering major, they're all like, really impressed because I'm a girl and I'm doing engineering." Notice that, in this case, the language is different; the Asian student's perception is that commentators are "impressed" not "surprised." Why might commentators be more impressed and not surprised with an Asian woman majoring in engineering? Some possible explanations might have to do with representation of Asian Americans and Latinas in engineering education— Asian American women have high levels of representation in engineering, while Latinas are underrepresented. Or perhaps the Asian American woman is more confident, therefore more impressive to commentators. Or perhaps the Latina misreads the commentator to infer that he or she was surprised to learn that she is majoring in engineering, rather than impressed—this could result from her own implicit biases about women in engineering. Another student adds that she longs for a future in which women in engineering are not anomalous:

> I would like it to be less shocking. . . . [O]utside of engineering school . . . people will just place just so much emphasis on the fact that you're a girl and that you graduated with an engineering degree. [T]hey automatically assume you're really smart, or you're intimidating . . . which is kind of cool, but at the same time I think it—I would like it to be a little more normal.

In the above quote, the student's use of the term "normal" reveals that her sense of belonging falls at the margins. Similar sentiments emerged in a different focus group by a White woman describing her experience on the first day of class: "[M]y section had two girls, and the first thing the teacher said was, 'Wow, there's two girls in the classes—most I've ever had. Never—all of my sections at [Institution Name]!'" In this example, the relative invisibility of women shifts with the presence of two women in one class, and the professor declares his surprise bringing attention to their atypical status as women in engineering.

Some Latinas described the sense of feeling excluded in terms of a double oppression, first as a woman, second as a person of color. Some women felt displaced when men asserted sentiments such as "you're only here because you are a woman." For women of color, this displacement is compounded by assumptions of being an affirmative action baby—highlighting not only subordinate status, but also a hint that they might not be academically qualified. In this example, a Latina student shares her response to such assumptions:

> In high school . . . my guy friends actually ended up going into engineering. [A] lot of them didn't get into [this institution], . . . they were very, well, jealous of it really [chuckles], because they really wanted to come here. [They would say] "You're a girl and you're Hispanic, and you're going into engineering. Dude, why would they not take you?" And I was like, "No, it's because my GPA is higher than yours, my SAT scores are higher than yours, and I'm more involved in school than you."

This Latina student explains how she has to establish her credentials because assumptions are made that she is unqualified based on her minority status as a woman of color in engineering. Another Latina had a similar experience. She related, "I'm in the honors program here. And one of my friends was like, well, the only reason you got in was because you're Hispanic. And I [thought], 'I do better than him in every single class, but somehow he is still better than me.'"

By contrast, Asian American women describe how they deal with the stereotype of being a model minority. The Asian American women unanimously agreed that there were expectations of high achievement imposed upon them by their teachers and peers: "[Y]ou must be smart, you must be good at math, or [others add 'Yeah']. It'd be like people always just set these expectations for you." Another woman added, "I feel like people sometimes have higher standards for Asians. . . . People treat you differently because of your race; I feel like there's just this standard of how Asians are smart and they can figure out this problem."

When probed about the effects of these stereotypes, there was an array of responses. Some Asian American women said that the stereotypes made them feel "stressed." Another added, "Sometimes it can either stress you out or motivate you." Some suggested the stereotype diminished at the college level, compared with the high school level (this may be because of the relatively higher critical mass of Asians in college). Most used humor to deflect the stereotype: "We're not especially smarter or whatever. I mean we used to joke about [it], like, 'Oh, that girl is Asian; she's smart. We can ask her a question.' But I mean we're just kidding. We know that's not really true" [others laugh, several: "Yeah"]. Here the implicit biases reflect societal stereotypes that Asians are smarter. Although this stereotype can lead to tremendous stress and pressure to succeed, we see in this example that the students use humor as a mode of resistance to make light of racial stereotypes, thereby diffusing their effects.

Some women suggested that at the interpersonal level, men in their academic work groups simply ignored them. One Latina student shared this narrative:

> Some guys they just don't listen to you. You're just a girl there and they don't even turn around to look at what you're saying. . . . At the beginning I was like, okay, probably he didn't listen to me—or he was concentrating. But then I realized that he was doing it on purpose. . . . He didn't even look at me. He didn't even say hi or anything. And a couple of times happened like that. . . . I felt bad. I felt very angry about it. But then I reacted like, okay, then he doesn't want to listen to me. So when he actually talked to me or answered, I did the same thing to him. I just didn't look at him, and I [thought], "Okay, do not look at him or anything." And then I think he realized it, because after that he actually came up to me one time, explaining and talked to me to my face and told me, "Oh look, um, I think, uh, we can do this and this and that." But still, I mean, we never said hi or anything like that. I've had other groups, after we have a group in a class, and you say "hi" to each other most of the time, because you see each other for several other classes.

This sense of invisibility was shared by another Latina student, who suggested that she is often ignored in group work. She laments that when the same response to a problem is proposed by a male student, then others listen:

> The one that comes to mind most is that when I've been in a group working— just last week we were studying for a P-chem [physical chemistry] test—it was

two boys and two girls, and we were all pretty lost in the subject. But, whenever a problem would come up, if the two guys were trying to work it out and one of the girls would offer some sort of suggestion—like I offered a suggestion to try to solve it—whenever the other guy said the same thing, it would just kinda like, all of a sudden click. I don't think they do it on purpose. It just—it shows.

Her deflated tone in the focus group, accompanied by her final comment, "it just shows," suggests that she sees the disparity in how she is treated by male students, even though she does not clearly articulate it as an injustice.

By contrast, this White female faced the same type of encounter but managed it differently:

I'm the person that would crack down on the guys when I was working with them because . . . they would disregard some of my ideas, and, um, it was a very tough thing because they, uh, were like, "You're a girl, you don't really know what you're talking about." And I never had encountered that before. It was one of the first situations I ever had seen that. So I really had to change my persona and kind of just become a different person in order to deal with that.

In this example, the student has adapted to the culture and says she "cracks down" on men. Her male peers, in this example, not only labeled her "girl," demoting her social status; they also negated her intellectual potential ("you don't know what you're talking about"). This White woman begins her narrative with a strong response about "cracking down" but also shares that she had to "change her persona" and "become a different person." We see from this comment that this student struggles to maintain her status in this hostile context, and even feels she has to change herself as a mechanism of adaptation. Even though White women share the same ethnicity with the majority of men, we see here that their gender is a delimiting social force among the boundaries of engineering.

Some Latinas complained about being made to serve in sex-typed roles during group work: "I've noticed that a lot of times, when I'm in working with a group with all guys, I'll get the secretary job." At this, several focus group students chuckle in unison. The student continues: "The men respond, 'That's because you're a girl.' What's that supposed to mean [chuckles], y'know? Like, because I'm a woman I can't participate in discussion?" Another Latina tries to explain it by excusing it as a socially male characteristic: "I think that they realize that somebody's talking when they actually hear us, but guys/boys . . . I dunno . . . probably because they're in engineering, I guess they understand each other better between guys, and they pay more attention to each other probably?" Another relates this to the overwhelming fact that it is predominately male, "probably because normally since the classes are mostly guys, and obviously the people, more people, doing well are gonna be guys, because, it's, uh, mostly guys." The students agree that, as one said, "Not every guy is like that." Still some suggest that they themselves internalize the effect of being among a minority, and are overwhelmed that they are outnumbered: "I'm kind of guilty in the same way. Like, if I need help, okay, I'm gonna [think] 'that guy is really smart.' Like, I don't say as many times, 'that girl is really smart.'" Another frames her response in the larger context of how women are portrayed in the media:

> Yeah, it's weird. I think it's mostly how we were raised, and the television that we watched. I feel like, yeah, I agree. I'll be doing my homework, and my best guy friend—I prefer to walk almost across campus to go ask him a question than to my roommate next door, because I feel like he gets it better.

Another adds,

> I don't know if it's necessarily because they're [men], but I think it's the people that speak up in class, you know, they're the ones asking questions, and you think, "Wow. They must be really smart." And because of the ratios in our classes, most of the time it is guys, so you make that connection that, you know, you make that connection that guys really are smarter than that girl. But I think it's because we're so outnumbered.

Insightfully, in this quote this Latina reflects that her own perceptions of who is smart germinate from who is most likely to speak openly in class. Given that the classes are primarily filled with men, this produces a particular effect—one that perpetuates the stereotype that men are smarter, faster at composing responses, and more confident in their intelligence. The perception of the women that men are "smarter" or better at technical topics echoes the influence of "stereotype threat" as discussed in Chapter 2. As a result of stereotype threat, women are less likely to have confidence in their own abilities; they second-guess themselves and take longer to produce answers.

These patterns of behavior reinforce false ideas about biologically determined intelligence, that men are innately more capable. The final Latina comment above suggests that this phenomenon emerges because of the large number of men compared to women. Women's voices are unheard because there are so few, thus stereotypes about who is capable, and who is not, are reproduced. A higher percentage of women would somewhat diffuse majority male voices. The situation can be so caustic for some women that they avoid group work altogether, as in this example:

> I've noticed that when I . . . go to professors for help—it's a much warmer environment I feel like, than if I go and work in groups, because when I work with groups, it just—it's a competitive—it just seems like a competitive environment. [Y]ou're working with groups, but nobody wants to give you their answers, nobody actually wants to explain it to you. They'll explain it to you,

but, I don't know—I just always found that when I went to the professors it
was a better environment than if I worked in a group.

This Latina student finds that seeking out the professor, rather than relying
on groups, is an effective strategy. This type of exclusion can be harmful
academically given the importance of group work in engineering education
and practice.

In focus groups, White women describe their perceptions of doing more
work than men; some students suggested that women need to do more to
combat the misperception that women were less capable: "I had to pretty
much step up because the guys weren't gonna do it. They were just gonna sit
there and let it fail. . . . I've noticed that the girls end up doing more work at
it than the guys do in the group projects. And, um, I think that's because
[men] know they can get away with it." Another student chimed in, "I think
girls care about their grades more [several focus group respondents agree]."

Institutional Microaggressions

Institutional microaggressions are the gendered and racially "marginalizing
actions and inertia of the university evidenced in structures, practices, and
discourses" that endorse a hostile campus climate" (Yosso, Smith, Ceja, &
Solórzano, 2009, p. 672). Institutional microaggressions are often invisible—
they seem "natural" given the history of the status quo in engineering. Students described instances in which their invisibility was heightened. A few
suggested that the discourse of their professors was gendered. Given the low
numbers of enrollment among women, some examples used by their professors exacerbate their relative isolation. In an example of a professor describing a mammogram, a White student shares that she was one of four women in
the class:

> I was sitting in the second row, and the professor's talking about how uncom-
> fortable a mammogram is and how it causes severe discomfort to women, and
> he was staring right at me the entire time [others all start laughing]. It was so
> awkward! He was just like staring right at me—making eye contact with me,
> talking about how you squish the breast [everyone laughing]. . . . He [said], "it
> can be really uncomfortable for a woman," and then just stares at me [laugh-
> ing].

In this example, the student feels the professor is marking her gender and
drawing attention to it in public. Although the professor may or may not have
been intentionally staring at her, the student is predisposed to assume that
given her low representation in the engineering program, any "feminine"
reference is an opportunity to tokenize her presence.

In industry, where students often do internships while in college, women work to strike a balance between defeating stereotypes (that brand them as bearers of gender, such as in the secretarial example) and being recognized as individuals (not as marginal subjects) with a valued identity. One White woman painfully shared a narrative in which her industry mentor told her to not be "giggly." This student had a deep, serious voice, appeared stoic in her mannerisms, and was reserved throughout the focus group interview. She described the following scenario:

> I thought about going to college to be an engineer, I knew that girls normally didn't do that. . . . It really didn't become an issue to me until actually, an internship the summer before I came here. I was working as a double-E [electrical engineering] intern as opposed to being a declared student. It was a major difference because I was the only girl in the office. And then I went back this past summer to work for the same company, and it was really weird, because my boss was a guy that graduated back—probably in the sixties or seventies. He's a much older gentleman, and he's never worked in the sense the way that we were working together, with a girl. Um, he'd had girls work around him and do like, you know, smaller tasks. But I was actually in there doing the jobs that a guy had been doing the summer before. And so it was really hard to prove myself to my employer, because we had to give a presentation. After the presentation he told me I was too giggly. And so . . . if a guy would have been up there giving the same presentation, he would have not thought that . . . [he] would have [said], "Good job," and stuff like that. As a woman in engineering, especially in the technical side, you're criticized more and expected to be more, I guess more manly than what most girls are.

In this example, the student describes how she was perceived by her internship manager as "giggly" and concludes that she has to appear more "manly." Her comments echo those of the other student presented earlier who described having to take on a different persona in working with men in academic groups. This student's narrative about her internship subtly hints at the tensions involved in working in a field in which women sense that their gender is so out of place that they must construct new gender norms for themselves, becoming more masculine, in order to fit in. This poses a burden for some women who must construct a new gender-coded script for themselves because they believe this will have a more positive effect on how they are treated in the field.

When Latinas were asked about stereotypes, they reflected in terms of gender, not ethnicity, and described stereotypes that emerge because of their low representation as women in engineering. One said, "I don't think that people look at me and automatically [think], 'she's dumb,' or, 'she won't be as good of an engineer.' I don't know, that's just how I feel." Another disagreed, "It just seems to me at least that there are some guys here that just get things. Like they don't spend any time outside class, you know, get an A on the test, and, whereas I spend hours upon hours outside of class getting to know the material. . . . My other friends that are girls, they do the same thing. We just—we just work at it, and I think sometimes guys have this gross stereotype that girls have to work at it a lot harder than guys do, and therefore . . . they think that they're more superior than you because they get it before you do." When asked by the Researcher, "And is that true, or is that a stereotype?" respondents had much to say about this. One added, "I think it's just a gross stereotype. I may not get it right away in class, but if I spend a few hours after class, I'll be able to understand it at the same level that you do." Another qualifies the response, "But I think that depends, because I've met—I've seen such smart girls in class . . . [Respondents murmur agreement] they get it just like that, even faster than guys. So the problem is that here we have so many guys, that of course [given] the amount of guys, you're going to have a higher number of guys getting it faster than a high number of girls getting it faster. [P]robably for every ten guys that get it faster, we only have one girl who gets it faster. That's because of the difference in the number of people. But I think it's just the same. If we had the same amount of girls as the same amount of guys that we have here, it'd be basically the same." Here we see that the women concur that perceptions of women's intelligence are affected by the low numbers of women. The fact that men are responding in greater numbers, more quickly, contributes to the stereotype that women are not as smart. Women are keenly aware of this numerical bias, and address it in terms of stereotypes that challenge them. Thus women here are articulating how the low numbers of women represented institutionally directly affect them through stereotypes. Further they realize these institutional effects will carry on into the workforce. One student commented, "Growing up with my mom as an engineer, I know that she, pay-wise, gets paid less than my dad, even though she handles bigger international projects, bigger projects than he does. She gets paid less than he does. So that's always been in back of my mind, [chuckles]. It's there, so . . ." In addition to experiencing tokenism, Latina engineering students acknowledge that a gender wage gap continues to reflect their subordinate status in the field of engineering. This topic is addressed further in the next section.

Jokes and Gendered Humor

Compounding their relative invisibility, women's subaltern status in engineering renders them as the butt of jokes. When Latinas were asked directly if they felt people in engineering should be more sensitive to issues of sexism, students described different issues related to jokes. One Latina student stated,

I just feel like I agree that [men] should be more sensitive. I feel like they need to admit it [chuckles]; a lot of guys we talked about still do it. They don't realize that they're doing it, or some do it on purpose because they believe [the stereotypes]. A lot of them joke about it, just socially in a social atmosphere. They'll just joke about, you know, they'll be sexists and it'll be "a joke." But it's really, it's not a, it's not a joke. It's not a joke. And, um, yeah, I think that they need be more sensitive—as in they need to realize that they're doing it, and realize that it's not true. We can do the same thing they can, so . . .

Another added,

Yeah, I think that it mainly concerns me when I think when [I'll] graduate as an engineer and, [I'll] be making less than a man, and it just doesn't really seem fair. I'm not going to say that's always going to happen, but it isn't even fair—at least if you look at our admissions, GPAs, women's GPA on campus in engineering is higher than the male GPA. And yes, there's fewer of us to pull from, but we're just as qualified as they are. We do the same work, and apparently we're a little bit better at it [chuckles] if we're having a higher GPA. And so I just don't think when people make jokes about that—it is a very sensitive issue—and it's not right.

Another agreed and added, "I also feel like women get paid less, [and] if you were to get paid more, they would just say you only got paid more because you were a girl, y'know? Another added, "That's always an excuse." [She and others chuckle, and add "Yeah."] "No matter what." As we can see in these quotes, when probed, Latina women grasp the broader ramifications stemming from the sexism embedded in jokes related to their presence in engineering. Latinas understand that what might be a joke to some can have real material disadvantages for them.

White women described how the mockery involves men laughing as they share stories of their sexual exploits with each other: "It really makes it hard for you to work with someone . . . when you know how they feel on certain situations, especially when it concerns sex basically." Another student adds, "I've heard some interesting things on the bus . . . and I'm the only girl on the bus!" Another woman adds, "I guess they just don't think that girls are listening." Chiming in, another White woman agrees,

Right, exactly. I mean, I've heard guys talking about how great a girl was in bed, or how awesome the blow-job he got last weekend was just right in front of me. Like, thinking nothing of the fact that I could be offended by this— talking about what a hot piece of ass this girl was. Like it's just really, really awkward and makes me uncomfortable—and kind of angry a lot. But I dunno—I just—it's like they don't realize that there's other genders there or that it can possibly be offensive.

Being exposed to sex talk and jokes was described by some as "disgusting" and "appalling." But one White woman explained how she took control of the situation: "I don't have to put up with guys doing it. . . . If they start talking about blow jobs or sex, I jump in. An' I'm like, 'yeah!' And then . . . I think I'm making them feel awkward. . . . I don't have to deal with it." Her advice to other women in engineering is: "If they're ever really bad, just jump in there and say something ridiculously vulgar, and you'll make them feel so out of place that they will shut up." While this student's narrative can be examined on multiple levels, what is clear is that she resists a potentially oppressive situation. She has learned to usurp men's sexual power by mocking it, and in this way she believes she has saved face and used an effective strategy to combat sexual harassment. The Latina and Asian women did not share similar narratives around sex jokes; they simply did not mention these, either because they were not salient in their everyday encounters or because they were not comfortable discussing such sensitive subjects. Among the White women, the topic emerged authentically—respondents were not asked specifically about jokes related to sex-themes.

ADAPTATION AND RESISTANCE TO MICROAGGRESSIONS

Women students have adopted a variety of strategies for being successful given the climate of microaggressions. Data analysis suggests these strategies vary by race. In some cases, women "claim empowerment from the margins" (Yosso, Smith, Ceja, & Solórzano, 2009) either by asserting themselves (by calling men out when they transgress) or by making accommodations to disengage and avert hostile situations (for example, skipping group work and meeting with the professor directly instead of engaging an indifferent male team). In this way, women students form "academic and social counterspaces" (Yosso, Smith, Ceja, & Solórzano, 2009) within the climate of engineering.

"Learning from Failure"

Latina women differed from other women in focus groups in their emphasis on "learning how to fail." Latinas explained that a key to persistence was adapting to the curve method of grading. One Latina explained her early frustrations in college: "You don't really understand . . . how classes are being curved. I just remember all in this college [and] crying to my mom, 'I'm going to fail! [chuckles]. Hope's going to be gone! I'll be home next semester! [giggles; joined by others]. Yes it is happening!'" Another said, "Learning to fail, learning that you're not good at everything. That was a huge shock to the system." Latinas in the focus group agreed that adjusting to curve grading and literally learning to fail was strategic to their persistence.

Latinas adapt to the climate in engineering education by attempting to carefully navigate setbacks. Some suggest that recognizing the problem is enough: "I guess when those things are going to happen to you, and when they happen, just ignore it, you know?" Another added the qualifier that it is valuable to draw on your own internal confidence: "Oh, yeah, and [know] that not everybody's like that. Just because you have one or two experiences, that doesn't mean that you can generalize. Because there are some good guys that really help you and they don't treat you like that. . . . It's not something to stress about. You know that you're smart, and just so long as you always remember that, that's enough." Another asserted the importance of standing up for oneself: "Don't be afraid to speak out, and [say] 'hold on a second!' Don't just sit there and let it happen. If you're in a group project, say some-thing—'Hold on, I think I'm right. I think I did this right.' That, uh, helps, I think." Here the student suggests the need to be confident and brave, but her hesitancy at the end of her assertion suggests that she herself is tentative about this proposition, and perhaps illustrates that such assertiveness is easier said than done. Hearing this, another respondent backed her up, "Yeah, be strong and don't be afraid or feel minimized because of that, because that doesn't really help. I mean that doesn't really affect you in the future to get a job or anything." Another student concurred, "Yeah, I was just going to say, speak up. Because most of the time when you're right, and you know you're right, guys will fight you until the end. They'll [say] 'no, I think you did this wrong.' So just stick with your guns, I guess." Viewed differently, as this Latina suggests, "sticking to your guns" is a warlike metaphor to suggest that it is a battlefield for some women. And yet, even with this powerful meta-phor, her assertion trails off with, "I guess," suggesting she is not convinced of this potential. In these subtle comments we perceive the complexity of being one of few Latina women in the classroom, and the difficulty in having the confidence to have faith in your own work, knowing that others may put you down even before they themselves do the work.

Experiences of "Pressure" among Latinas

Latinas also described pressures they put on themselves, as well as pressures they sense from their family, even extended-family, members. For example, one student said, "I think I put a lot of pressure on myself. I feel like I'm very competitive, and I always want to do the best [among] everyone I study with; I like to do better than them on all the tests. It's just my nature I guess [chuckles]." Another concurred but expanded her comments to include her larger family: "Yeah, I agree with her. It's pressure I put on myself, but also pressure from my family I guess. Um, my parents were the first ones to go to college. And then my cousins in my generation all went to college, and . . . they're all lawyers and journalists . . . none of them are engineers. . . . I guess my parents expect me to stick up for them. It'd be like, um, yeah, we're good engineers too, and [can] succeed like they did." Here we see that this Latina, as the first in her family to go to college, feels competition with her successful, college-educated cousins. Therefore, her own pressure to succeed is measured against the success of her relatives, and stems from a desire to make her parents look good in the larger context of her family.

Another Latina, by contrast, disagreed:

> I wouldn't say it's from my parents. Both my parents were actually accountants, so they're kind of happy that I've decided to do something different. But I think the main issue that I have is my other family members. . . . They put a lot of pressure on me, not purposely, but they'll go tell their families, oh, "Penelope [pseudonym]—she's at [Name of University]. She's doing so well." And then I think, oh man, what if I don't do well? What are they [chuckles] gonna be tellin' the family? "Oh, did you hear about Penelope and how she is failing at life?" [Others chuckling] I'm sure it would never happen, but I just don't want to disappoint them. They're so proud of you, and you're afraid, "God, if I do something wrong, or if I don't meet their expectations, they're not gonna be as proud of me," and I just feel like that would really upset me.

In this example, we see that the Latinas view themselves as representatives for their family, and perhaps for their community, and they interpret this as a responsibility that extends beyond themselves. One student shared the following narrative:

> My parents, they both went to college, but my mom was an economics major. My dad was initially entered as a mechanical engineering major, but then he switched over to business. And so neither of them have done engineering, but they've both kind of pushed it—not pushed it on me by any means, but whenever I said that I wanted to be an engineer, they [said], "That's a good major. It's a global major, math is not gonna change anywhere you go." And since we had to move here, [they said] "If you ever have to move anywhere else, it's easy to understand numbers anywhere you go, but economics can change, and the way you do business changes." And they'll tell all their friends like that, so—I mean, it's not they're telling me to get a 4.0 [GPA] or anything, but you don't want to come back and fail out of school or something, because they wouldn't have anything to talk about.

In this example, Latinas understand that their parents view their engineering major as a source of pride, and this affects them at a personal level, both as a source of support and a source of stress. Another concurred, "Yeah, I'm the same way. My parents don't pressure me, but it is the same thing. I pressure myself because, man, I want to graduate. I want to have a good GPA, and because of all the effort that they've done for me to come here. But, they're very happy. None of them are engineers. They think the same way, that math is universal—you can go anywhere with it, and that it's a good major."

These internal and external pressures affect how students describe a sense of balance in their lives, and their coping strategies. Our focus groups were limited to women who were persisting in engineering; some students switch majors early on. As one Latina noted, "People will drop like flies your freshman year and they say, 'Oh well, I switched to management, I took the M Train.'" And another adds, "Because it so much easier." But among those who persist, the road is not always smooth. They describe isolation, depression, and obsessive behavior as common territory for engineering students. Much of these responses are due to the competitive environment in engineering.

In talking about competition, Latina students framed comments in a wider context of the academic climate. For some, the context produced consequences that affected the way they experienced student life. For example, one Latina shared this narrative:

> In my freshman year socially, it was pretty warm. As freshmen you're all really excited because it's college, and you get to meet new people and if you're a freshman coming in, then everyone's kind of in the same boat. But I think, academically, it's pretty cold. Everyone's really competitive within your major [two other participants say "That's true"]. Everyone is after the same internships, after the same jobs. Like if it comes to getting a lab position, and if you're doing research in a lab, then everyone's after that same lab. Everyone wants to get in a good lab. Maybe it'll get warmer as I get into senior year, but I think it's pretty chilly right now [chuckles].

Another concurred,

> Yeah, actually . . . there are a lot of people who will help you out and give you the solution so you can look at it and do it together. But a lot of students [say] "these are mine" [someone says "Yeah"] and it's curved, based on what everyone gets [others start voicing agreement. "Yeah. Uh-huh"]. So everyone [says], "Oh, don't give this old test to that person because then it'll make the average grade go up, and then it'll be harder for us." [Others say "Yeah."]

For one Latina, the consequence of this competition was a sense of isolation, a sense of not having friends in her major.

> I remember when I transferred. At first I didn't know anybody. I think I lost like ten pounds in my first semester. It was shocking. My first time being away from home, plus when I got here, I didn't know anybody, and seeing how competitive people were, so I was kind of competitive at the beginning. But then it really got me to the point that I'm like, "I don't want to be like these people." People are so competitive that it gets to a point that you cannot really make friends, good friends, real friends. I mean I don't have any good friends in my major. The good friends I have, they're from different majors. Even within your major, like the girls that you see, some Latin girls, they're even

competitive with you. And it's kinda hard, the competition. I mean, I remember there was this company that came to talk to us at [a professional society] meeting. They made this competition, and they made everybody stand up. They said, "Okay, people who have a 3.8 GPA and above, sit down. People who have a 3.7 GPA and above, sit down," and things like that. And so they had this iPod as a gift. And that gift was going to go to the person with the lowest GPA. So that iPod actually went to the person with a 2.5 GPA or something like that. And what they said was something like, "We're not really looking for your GPA. We know you're at [this great university]. We know you're capable of critical thinking, we know you're capable of thinking and doing stuff." And I really liked that. And that's probably when I opened my eyes and I [thought], I don't want to be competitive anymore, because you can be competitive to yourself, but not to anybody else, y'know? Try to make things for yourself, but not just because you want to be better than her, or you want to be better than the other one. You know it is just for you, and then if you cannot accomplish it, you did your best for yourself, not just because you don't want her or him to be better than you. And some people kind of twisted that because they want to get good grades and all of that, and it gets to the point they don't realize that sometimes they're doing it just because that person is doing it. And sometimes they push themselves up to a point that they don't enjoy different things of life. I mean, we're still young, and there's some people out there that . . . it's hard to make friends like that. I mean that's my point of view. People are very competitive here.

Another added,

Most of my friends are not engineering students. Yeah, I socialize with engineering students in my classes, but outside I'm mostly friends with people that are not engineers. This is probably a gross stereotype, but they just want to talk about school and classes, "What did you get on that test?" And like, when I'm out of class, I don't want to talk about school [chuckles]. I want to talk about, you know, what happened in the latest episode of *Grey's Anatomy*, something like that [she and others chuckling]. Like, I don't want to talk about school.

Another adds, "Most of the people here just talk about classes instead." Another concurs, "Yeah, you'll meet them at a party, and then [chuckles] they'll be like, 'Oh, class . . . that test was so hard!' And you're like, 'Are you serious?' [She and others laughing]. 'It's Friday night and we're both drinking, an' you're telling me about the test' [laughs]." Another exclaims, "I'm like, 'What is this—we're at the party! Why can't we just . . .?'"

Latina women describe their social life as bracketed between students with whom they can talk about their academics versus "real friends." This contrasts with the White women's narratives in our focus groups who described mixing academic and social spaces and having friends within their majors. This gives them less of a sense of being outsiders, but exposes them to sexism and sexist jokes. White women also reported joining societies for social and academic opportunities (i.e., Society of Women Engineers [SWE], Women in Engineering [WIE], sororities). Latinas reported being more likely to join engineering societies that offer support to women of color (such as Society for Hispanic Professional Engineers [SHPE]). However, they cite professional development, not social opportunities, as the most likely reason for joining. The idea of having one peer group for academic interactions and one for social interactions was also found by researchers for women of color in college (Justin-Johnson, 2004; Tate & Linn, 2005, cited in Espinosa, 2009) including Latinas (Ortiz, 1986). Since academic peer support has been found to be an important contributor to persistence (Espinosa, 2009), the difficulty in finding such support is problematic for Latinas.

Much of the competition is structural. Some professors organize the class to enhance the competitive context. This Latina describes how it affected her:

> When I came in as a freshman, our Calculus II class, it was a very competitive class, and [the professor] told us it was competitive. I mean he told us, "you know, it's every man for themselves" and, [chuckles] I got into that mess. And I [thought] okay, well, I can't help so-and-so because then she might get a higher grade than me. And it was horrible, and it was terribly lonely [another participant says "Yeah"], and, yeah, I did well, but was it really worth it? You know, you just don't make any friends, and so I've kind of geared more towards group work [but] I kind of steer clear of groups, only because it just seems like, professors nowadays are really trying to get the cheating thing, so I've kind of avoid working with groups, because sometimes they consider group collaboration cheating.

They also describe how the teachers are stratifying the class grading system, and how this affects competition:

> A lot of the teachers, they [say] "I only want 10 percent As." And at the beginning of the semester in the syllabus there is a grade distribution. This top whatever percent get A's, this percent gets B's, this is how I'm gonna curve. I overheard a professor talking to a TA. The test [average] was a ninety-something or high eighty. And the professor [said], "Okay, then we have to make it more challenging. And so professors are always looking —even if they cover the material or whatever, if the class [does well], they always try to make it more challenging and more challenging and more challenging.

Another adds, "I think that's what fuels our competitiveness. We all want to do well. It's sometimes hard to know what the professor's thinking, because everyone will do well on the test, and then they'll [say], 'Well, it wasn't hard enough!' And you'll [say], 'No! That means we learned it! That means we got it!' [Others all start chiming in at once. Several 'Yeahs' and some chuckling.] That means we got it! It doesn't mean it was easy!"

Adjustments professors make to grades will also affect competition among students. Grade inflation was a common theme: "The teachers think it's okay to give a test, and the average is going to be 50%, [another Latina interjects 'Yeah, I heard that'] and they think that that's all right [Others talking all at once; heard 'Yeah' and 'No!' and 'As if that's okay!'] and that's their goal [chuckles] really every time." Another adds, "Why are you going to give a test if your average is 50 and then you are going to curve around that? Why don't you just give a test . . . a regular test, so we all get normal grades? I just don't get it [chuckles]."

The competitive climate creates an environment in which students find little time to rest. Some students describe it as rewarding, as in this example: "Those classes are really impossible and harsh and everything. Then you look at your grade, and once your grades come in, you know you did it. I guess it's a sense of pride." Others by contrast lament the workload: "I envy a lot of my friends. They'll [say], 'what're you doing on a Sunday?' They call you. 'What are you doing?' Oh, I'm working on a project. They're like, 'What?!?' [Others chuckling] 'It's Sunday!' I say, yeah, well, here every day is the same day [chuckling], Monday through Sunday, every day is the same thing. If you got stuff to do, you gotta do it." Other Latinas also compare themselves to nonengineering friends: "To me it's the end goal. I have friends that went to other colleges, and they're cruisin' through however many hours they're taking. They're able to watch six hours of TV a day! [others start chuckling] And you're working hard. And you think to yourself, well you know what? When I graduate, I might have a lower GPA than them, but I have [this University's name]. And I think it's that name I survived, [chuckling], and I can conquer the world."

"You Are on Your Own"

Latinas describe an extreme sense of individualism in engineering education. One student contrasted the experience with her former community college:

> [Here] you are on your own. Me being a Latin person, [typically] we Latins help each other. At my former campus, we'd always help each other. We'd be more social, have more friends—different interaction. And so you come here, it's just you—people are so competitive that you're on your own, and even people tell you that, "Try to find things on your own. Try to do things on your own. You've got to do it yourself." And it's true, I learned that. But it gets to a point that *everything* is on your own, so you're on your own. You grow up on your own, you don't make any friends . . . Sometimes you [feel you] have to share something, some of your knowledge. So I guess that's been the hardest part for me to overcome. And the way I did it, at the beginning, I learned how to do everything. I mean, do my own research even though I would spend hours overnight—pull a lot of overnighters—no choice. And then eventually you actually get to know, a little bit, more different people, so you know who

to deal with, who to interact with. But that doesn't happen just like that, because some people are so quiet that they don't even talk to you or anything.

Another adds,

After I started being so competitive I actually got to know more people because I realized that . . . I mean, I'm a young person. And you don't know what is going to happen tomorrow, and so you realize that you spend all [these] hours just studying, just on your own, and you're like, okay, this is not right. I mean this is five years of your life—probably the best five years. You could enjoy and have friends because after that you will be working full-time. And now things have changed. Now I'm going to try to balance everything out.

But this balance is difficult and Latinas describe how it can differently affect students. One student relates how her campus had among the highest rates of depression among college students in the nation: "The students are most miserable here." Another adds, "I've had a lot of friends that have had to withdraw from classes, not go to class, a few really close friends had to withdraw from classes, stop taking classes next semester, go on medication, because they've been depressed." Another adds, "It's a serious issue here." One student shared a personal narrative related to how the stress and isolation affected her personally:

My first semester I was taking four classes and it got to a point that I lost so much weight that I would talk to my family, and they would [say], "You know what? Just take it easy. They would tell me, you know what? Just take it easy and drop one class." It got to a point that I would be up doing stuff because the professors don't have time, they don't help you. I don't know anybody, so I'd be up all the way up to five in the morning, six in the morning, trying to do a project without eating. Because if you get out of the lab, you couldn't get in. And the software was in the lab. I didn't have it on my laptop. Now we can get into our buildings any time during the night. You get out, you go eat, and then you come back. But my first semester we didn't have that, so we had to stay late. If you had a friend, you could go and come back, but in some cases you didn't.

Another adds, "The library gets so packed that if you move, you lose yourself a spot." The work ethic in engineering is inculcated during the earliest years in the baccalaureate program. This work ethic involves working lengthy hours to complete weekly homework assignments or "problem sets" and projects. Hard work is prized in the students' engineering culture creating what Stevens, Amos, Garrison, and Jocuns (2007) call a "meritocracy of difficulty." The cumulative nature of the engineering material means that students must keep up a constant high level of effort and focus on problem sets rather than lengthy readings and less structured periods of intense research and writing prior to deadlines, as may be the case in humanities or social science courses with fewer major papers.

Our findings demonstrate that Latina engineering students continue to experience many of the same challenges faced by women and yet respond in unique ways. This work demonstrates a pattern across geographic location and through time as our findings are consistent with those of Hacker (1989), Seymour and Hewitt (1997), and Tonso (2007) beginning decades ago.

CONCLUSION

In this chapter, we conducted a case study of Latina undergraduate engineering by using focus group data. Their narratives were contrasted with data collected from other focus groups of women of diverse racial backgrounds. In our analysis, we draw on a framework of microaggressions as a lens to understand how women perceive the academic and social climate of engineering education. Women respond and adapt in various ways to a variety of interpersonal and institutional microaggressions as well as jokes, depending on their race/ethnicity. Their unique perspectives shed light on the microstrategies and counterspaces that emerge as mechanisms for coping in an environment that can be competitive, isolating, and sometimes demoralizing. More research is needed to understand how social class differences, and parental influence, affect pathways into engineering.

Chapters 3 and 4 used mixed methods (both quantitative and qualitative) to understand the obstacles and pockets of potential for Latina engineering students. In Chapter 5, we turn to practical strategies that have been successful in breaking barriers for Latinas in higher education and a broader vision for engineering education. We also review curricular and extracurricular programming that affects persistence among Latina engineering students. We describe how educators, administrators, and mentors can continue to support Latina students as they navigate the academic environments that lead to pathways in engineering.

Chapter Five

Crossing Borders

Opportunities and Challenges

How can Latino and Latina students be reached? In this chapter, we argue that recruiting Latinas into engineering is intimately tied with breaking barriers within education. Systemic problems plague Latino communities, including stratified schools with differential access and opportunities. Broader social inequities including poverty and institutional racism also persist as structural barriers for Latinos in education. To help Latinos/as succeed in higher education in general, Nevarez (2001) highlights secondary school preparation, postsecondary institutional climate, financial aid and tuition, and access to information about college. To fulfill the potential of Latinas in engineering, in this chapter, we propose radical systemic changes as well as targeted intervention and recruiting strategies:

- Re-envisioning engineering: moving it from the borderlands into the core.
- Enhancing classroom climate through innovative pedagogical strategies.
- Revitalizing the content of engineering curricula.
- Pursuing recruitment opportunities at community colleges, particularly at Hispanic-serving institutions (HSIs).
- Creating intensive precollege academic preparation, particularly in math and science.
- Expanding outreach beyond the individual student.
- Establishing and sustaining social support, networking opportunities, and mentors/role models.
- Redefining engineering in ways that are meaningful to Latino youth.

RE-ENVISIONING ENGINEERING

Over the last few decades, there have been numerous and valiant efforts to enhance the diversity of the engineering and STEM workforce and educational population. Despite these efforts, diversity in engineering has not changed significantly with the percentages of women of all races and African American, Latino, and Native American men remaining essentially constant. Such stasis points to the need for significant fundamental change. As Heywood argues, most reform efforts have operated within a *convergent framework* where the past is seen as a guide to the future resulting in incremental changes (2012a). To enact meaningful change, he advocates for *divergent visioning* as a more promising strategy. Others have called for revolutionary educational reform (Busch-Visniac & Jarosz, 2004; Lucena, 2005). We agree that revolutionary divergent visioning is needed—the field of engineering education cannot remain a segregated elite enclave.

The re-envisioning of engineering, we argue, should include sweeping modifications to existing curricula with the intent of moving engineering off of the borderlands of education. Currently, engineering is largely absent from K–12 education. Exposure to and preparation for engineering must happen at the earliest levels of education. Doing so ensures that engineering will be familiar to young people, Latinas included, so that they can be recruited early, enveloped in the process of understanding the field, and guided toward pursuing engineering as a career. There are hopeful signs in this regard, particularly the promise of new science standards in K–12 education in California that will include engineering for the first time (Pham, 2011). These are based on a framework developed by the National Research Council (2011) with the goal to

> ensure that by the end of 12th grade, all students have some appreciation of the beauty and wonder of science, the capacity to discuss and think critically about science-related issues, and the skills to pursue careers in science or engineering if they want to do so—outcomes that existing educational approaches are ill-equipped to achieve.

Such promising efforts have the potential to lift barriers of access to engineering. Together with other educational reforms, such curricular revisions will open new doors to young students.

Engineering as Part the "Core" of Liberal Arts in the 21st Century

Since this book focuses on higher education where engineering education is situated today, we will focus on recommendations for higher education. Broadly, our proposal is that engineering should become a part of the core of the education of all college-educated students. Several leaders have called for the need for engineering to be recognized as part of the essential education of an educated person in the 21st century in the tradition of liberal arts. In today's world, engineering should not be the purview of a small minority. Given our societal infusion with ever-increasing technological capacities, a greater majority must share, understand, and begin to shape it. As Carol Christ, president of Smith College, declares,

> Traditional definitions of the liberal arts often claim a dichotomy between general knowledge—appropriately the province of the liberal arts—and knowledge that is professional, technical, or useful. That dichotomy is a false one. . . . Indeed, engineering must become part of a liberal education in the 21st century. We must determine not only how best to educate engineers in the traditional liberal arts but also what role engineering might play in the education of musicians, economists, political scientists, and philosophers. Just as the study of literature and art enriches and deepens the education of scientists and engineers, so the study of science and engineering should enrich and deepen the education of historians and poets. . . . [E]ngineering is inherently interdisciplinary, using a broad range of knowledge in science and mathematics to develop solutions to many of today's problems. It is both research- and project-based, providing multiple opportunities for students to solve new problems under the guidance of faculty and industry mentors. The practice of engineering is international, as engineers work without borders, yet its goals are profoundly civic: engineers use their knowledge in service of society, responding to human needs and problems with technological solutions. Engineering also embraces sustainability as a core value—indeed, in a world of finite natural resources, we depend upon it, engineering, to conserve the resources that sustain us. (*Chronicle of Higher Education*, 2008)

The convergence of multidisciplinary sectors, across both intellectual and nation-state borders, provides rich possibilities for enhanced understanding of social problems. As our technological productions and knowledge become increasingly transnationally shared (Esparragoza, Larrondo-Petrie, Jordan, & Saavedra, 2007; Larrondo-Petrie, Otero Gephardt, & Esparragoza, 2012), a broader swath of participants, including teachers, business professionals, and social scientists, must be included in the process of generating and educating society about scientific and engineering matters.

There is a critical need for informed, technically literate citizens. Robert L. Clark, dean of the School of Engineering and Applied Sciences at the University of Rochester, explains:

> The world's greatest challenges—for example, the need for water and energy in the greater context of environmental responsibility—cry out for a technically literate society, capable of creating solutions and communicating effectively to influence public policy. (*Chronicle of Higher Education*, 2008)

For example, many young people today are interested in "green energy" but do not realize that engineering is a critical part of these endeavors. As society increases its political awareness of the importance of environmental problems, engineering offers the capacity to understand social problems through an interdisciplinary lens. Nevertheless, few students immediately see the connections between environmental challenges and engineering solutions. Given student contemporary interest in solving ecological and environmental problems, potential exists for attracting students to engineering through this angle. Recent research shows that the highest percentage of women *faculty members* in any engineering subdiscipline is in environmental engineering (Yoder, 2011).

More broadly, H. Vincent Poor, dean of the School of Engineering and Applied Science at Princeton University, argues that knowledge of science and technology is fundamental to a well-rounded education:

> Today no one should consider her or himself to be well-educated without knowing something about science and technology—not specialized knowledge, but a basic familiarity with principles and a recognition that science and technology flow throughout our culture, even dominating many aspects of our lives. (Poor, 2007)

Faculty and academic leaders need to be champions in re-envisioning the core. As institutions reflect on and modify their mission statements, they should consider their role in meeting the needs of students in an ever-changing technological world:

> The role of educational institutions—which has been more or less constant since classical times—has been to engage the next generation, to bring them along intellectually and to help them move into leadership positions. Of course, times change and the subject matter that we teach certainly changes. Today more than ever, any leader must be comfortable thinking about scientific and technological subjects: What are the basic principles behind current developments? How have technology and society shaped each other at key moments through history? (Poor, 2007)

Such questions reveal the interdisciplinary character of engineering, and its mutual role in producing in societal change. As educational institutions chart the future of our nation's leadership and global interconnections, competence and authority in addressing these issues rests on a broad, interdisciplinary base of knowledge. As John Heywood (2012b) asserts,

> [E]ngineering literacy is necessarily inter-disciplinary and a liberal study. Through the production of a design a student is brought face to face with the social purposes and consequences of technology, the practice of manufactur-

ing, the management of people, and the personal transferable skills required that are demanded by continually changing patterns of work.

This literacy transcends academic boundaries and should reach into its current borderlands. Heywood warns of the danger of specialist education and general education that does not include technology. Heywood also explains that such knowledge is critical for employment for all students and ties this to lifelong learning and adaptability throughout one's career.

Engineering has recognized the importance of liberal arts in the education of undergraduate engineers. A liberal arts complement is part of the requirements for engineering accreditation under ABET. The curriculum, however, is seldom integrated. Rather, the liberal arts are considered the domain of certain faculty, and engineering that of others. Such silos do not help faculty or students to learn from each other. If engineering moves out of the borderlands of education and into the core, there are implications for all faculty. Also, this should be a reciprocal arrangement: engineering faculty and students need to be more broadly educated; similarly those in other fields (social science, science, arts, and humanities) need to possess engineering/technical literacy so that they can work together to solve interdisciplinary problems.

Impact on Engineering Faculty

For engineering faculty, re-envisioning engineering as part of the core brings with it a responsibility to develop courses that appeal to students across campus. This involves reaching outside of comfort zones to develop courses that will attract students and provide broad introductions. Engineering faculty typically teach required classes that need no marketing or promotion, so this presents a new challenge. Some of the introduction to engineering courses for first-year students might be adapted for this purpose, but most cannot be used without modification. Partnerships with faculty outside of engineering could be particularly valuable here. This could take many forms, with examples of models including team-taught courses or modules with engineering and nonengineering faculty teaching together, paired courses between engineering and another discipline, and engineering faculty teaching core courses. Design is a critical aspect to incorporate in such classes because it is fundamental to the field. The engineering design process itself achieves multiple learning objectives from innovation to critical thinking along with a myriad of other professional and technical skills. The goal of such courses would not be to have every student become an expert in engineering. Rather, "an informed understanding of how engineers conceptualize, create, and evaluate could help other scholars expand or refine their own thinking and paradigms" (*Chronicle of Higher Education*, 2008) and help to regenerate the field of engineering.

Examples of such an approach are the integrated curricula for engineering students (primarily used with first-year engineering students) combining topics in engineering, physics, chemistry, and English. A review of these programs is provided by Froyd and Ohland (2005), who define these as curricula in which (a) faculty members from multiple disciplines collaborate to develop and implement the curriculum, (b) assessment data is reported on specific outcomes that result from the curriculum, and (c) students enroll in courses from different disciplines or in a course that combines multiple disciplines. Results from these integrated curricula have shown that they are beneficial for student learning and appeal more than traditional curricula to underrepresented groups in engineering (Froyd & Ohland, 2005). Despite these benefits, however, integrated curricula have not become widespread in engineering education, primarily due to the structural barriers in traditional academic institutions that impede working across departmental boundaries. More radical transformations are needed at the macro level such as via the accreditation body, ABET.

Impact on Faculty Outside of Engineering

For faculty outside of engineering, re-envisioning engineering as part of the core brings with it the need to recognize engineering as a legitimate part of academia and to engage with engineers so that they are in a position to educate students more broadly. Do liberal arts faculty agree with or embrace the idea that engineering belongs in the core of liberal arts or even in the academy? In the *Chronicle of Higher Education*, Carol Christ describes the unexpected benefits that engineering can have on other areas of the curriculum:

> Faculty members have commented on the ethical seriousness that engineers bring to classes in history, or literature, or philosophy; they come with an awareness that solutions to complex problems, in whatever discipline, are best considered in a broad context, including their ethical implications. Moreover, the engineering program's focus on collaborative work and public-presentation abilities have inspired renewed interest in developing such capacities in students across each of the academic divisions. Similarly intriguing to other faculty members is the engineering program's use of portfolios to assess students' abilities and document students' growth as they mature in their field of study. (2008)

The contributions of engineering faculty, particularly recent pedagogical innovations, have the potential to be translated into multiple fields. Methodologically and pedagogically, there are points of convergence where engineers can add value.

INNOVATIVE PEDAGOGICAL STRATEGIES
IN ENGINEERING EDUCATION

Traditional engineering education has changed little in the last few decades in terms of pedagogy and content. Efforts to change have been motivated by "rewards" such as funding from the National Science Foundation (NSF) and "punishments" such as ABET accreditation requirements. For example, to address the serious retention problem of first-year engineering matriculants, coalitions of universities, funded by NSF, successfully developed creative, design-based introduction to engineering courses to provide valuable context to complement the standard math, physics, and chemistry offerings. By contrast, the widespread incorporation of learning objectives, arguably fundamental to effective education, is the mandated result of ABET requirements. Both sets of structural changes slowly continue to chip away at the rigid format of engineering curricula. Below we review some promising changes in pedagogy such as more collaborative and active learning, teamwork, and community service learning. All of these could be beneficial for all students including Latinas. In addition, culturally responsive teaching and targeted approaches that address gendered and raced inequities may be helpful. Finally, reimagining the structural format and content itself of engineering curricula yields possibilities for radical change.

Promising Efforts: Innovative Pedagogy

Collaborative and active learning have gained popularity in engineering and have been shown to be effective (Prince, 2004; Prince & Felder, 2006; Smith, Sheppard, Johnson, & Johnson, 2005). These pedagogies embrace what has been termed the "social dimension of learning" (Bransford, Vye, & Bateman, 2004), rather than focusing only on transmitting content unilaterally. Espinosa's findings for women of color in undergraduate STEM (2009) suggest the need to support a model of student empowerment that draws on a socially engaged learning praxis. She argues that much of this work is in line with

> practices set forth by feminist scholars and theories of learning specific to women: encouraging students to question the role of power in the creation of scientific knowledge, aligning theoretical concepts with real-world scientific problems and experiences (e.g. economic, social, environmental), integrating problem-based learning, and increased interpersonal collaboration amongst students inside the classroom. (2009, p. 142)

Scholars in engineering education are exploring the incorporation of feminist and liberative pedagogy into engineering education (Beddoes, 2012; Eschenbach, Cashman, Waller, & Lord, 2005; Lord & Camacho, 2007a, 2007b; Pawley, n.d.; Riley, 2003, 2012). These practices are beneficial for *all* students but particularly beneficial for women and students of color, who may feel disenfranchised in what has been termed the "chilly" classroom (Sandler, Silverberg, & Hall, 1996).

Teamwork is an essential aspect of engineering practice and a critical component in teaching engineering. Research has identified issues that arise in teams based on gender and race (Cordero, DiTomaso, & Farris, 1997; Heller & Hollabaugh, 1992; Kirchmeyer, 1993; Rosser, 1998). Best practices based on this research (that prevent the isolation of women and minorities on teams) have been incorporated into an award-winning and widely used electronic aid for team formation in engineering, the Comprehensive Assessment of Team Member Effectiveness (CATME) (Ohland, Pomeranz, & Feinstein, 2006). An instructor's awareness of such issues is critical for broadening participation of Latinas in engineering.

Community Service Learning (CSL) has proven to be an effective pedagogy within engineering education (Coyle, Jamieson, & Oakes, 2005; Tsang, 2000). CSL offers possibilities for peer mentoring if college students work with younger students in schools (Lord, 2000). CSL could be particularly beneficial for Latino students in bridging classroom and community particularly for universities physically located in or near communities with large Latino populations such as HSIs (see Camacho, 2004). Participating in such service or mentoring has been correlated with a greater sense of belonging in college for Latino students (Delgado Bernal, Alemán, & Garavito, 2009; Hurtado & Carter, 1997).

Acknowledging Structural Challenges: Culturally Responsive Pedagogy

Specific efforts that acknowledge the structural inequities, and institutional biases, that Latino/a students face are imperative. Pappamihiel and Moreno (2011) advocate for culturally responsive teaching (CRT) at the university level as an extension of culturally relevant pedagogy in K–12. They propose that such efforts may be particularly helpful for promoting the success of Latinos in predominantly White institutions (PWIs). Given the large number of PWIs that grant engineering degrees, this is particularly important for engineering. Their goal is to "help scaffold students into a more integrated community of learners" (Pappamihiel & Moreno, 2011, p. 333). They emphasize that academic expectations still remain high but CRT can help foster egalitarian conditions through efforts such as true instruction accommodations, clear objectives, and acknowledgement of culture differences and the fact that these might impact how students learn. CRT can be empowering, validating, and combat isolation students feel. They also hope "that CRT could be used not only to improve academic outcomes and retention, but also as a coping strategy to influence students who are experiencing 'ethnic evasion'" (2011, p. 341). CRT has an emancipatory and transformative aspect as well: "By empowering Latino students within a university setting, they allow students to become part of the system that may have previously been an agent of discrimination against them or their families" (2011, p. 336). Outside of class, assigning team research projects encourages students to bring their perspectives into the classroom. If such projects have a culturally relevant focus, the work can build leadership skills, allowing students to make a deeper connection with course material.

Culturally responsive teaching might help instructors recognize strengths of Latinos that could be beneficial in engineering. For example, Pappamihiel and Moreno (2011) posit that university professors may be able to

> take advantage of the social aspects that are appreciated by many Latino cultures. In a variety of Latino cultures, stage-setting, and context-creation are essential aspects of problem-solving. University professors often disregard this aspect of problem-solving in the directness of American culture. However, this ability to look at a problem holistically is an aspect of many Latino cultures that could benefit many American students. . . . By taking advantage of the context-creation and establishing prior knowledge of a problem-solving task, professors can set the stage of an academic task and allow all students to view its multiple perspectives. (2011, pp. 335–336)

This may be particularly valuable for engineering, where these ideas relate to several aspects of the engineering design process, including (1) defining the problem, which is the first and arguably the most important step, and (2) appreciating the social impact of engineering solutions. The engineering accreditation body, ABET, includes several undergraduate student outcomes that are relevant here (ABET, 2012a):

> (c) an ability to design a system, component, or process to meet desired needs within realistic constraints such as economic, environmental, social, political, ethical, health and safety, manufacturability, and sustainability;
> (f) an understanding of professional and ethical responsibility;
> (h) the broad education necessary to understand the impact of engineering solutions in a global, economic, environmental, and societal context.

Pappamihiel and Moreno explain that CRT is "as much about knowing yourself and how your culture and identity can impact someone else as it is about knowing someone else's culture and ethnic identity" (2011, p. 333). Since engineering education is only recently coming to grips with the idea of an engineering culture and what that means (Godfrey & Parker, 2010), utilizing CRT is a large challenge. This does require instructors to recognize the various identities of their students and to create a safe community within the classroom. It is encouraging that there are engineering faculty who place a high value on developing community in the classroom. In a study of engineering educators who attended the *Frontiers in Education (FIE)* conference in 2006, researchers found that "building a sense of community in the classroom" was one of the top three teaching practices for participants (Lord & Camacho, 2007b).

At the college level, research has shown that creative pedagogical approaches have shown promise for recruiting and retaining Latino students in engineering. With a wider pool of Latino engineering matriculants, such efforts may become even more critical. A shift in pedagogical approaches to increase the design and teamwork aspects of their curriculum is beneficial for Latinos (Besterfield-Sacre, Moreno, Shuman, & Atman, 2001). A notable example is work from the University of Colorado (Carlson & Sullivan, 2004; Knight, Carlson, & Sullivan, 2003). Researchers there found a remarkable 54% retention improvement for Latino engineering students who took their First Year Engineering (FYE) class compared with those who did not. They also saw a 27% retention improvement for women. In this FYE class, students worked in teams to design, build, and test prototypes while also working on developing oral and written communication skills. Key aspects of this effort that contributed to its success included opportunities for hands-on work, exposure to design, fostering personal relationships between students on small teams, and working on "real-world" projects such as low-tech solutions to problems in developing countries. Such features might be easy to incorporate into various classes and might be particularly valuable for Latino students in making them feel more welcome in engineering and helping them to see connections between engineering and solving socially relevant problems.

To be truly transformative, efforts to reform the engineering curriculum should be mindful of the raced and gendered cultural context in which engineering education exists (see Chapter 2). A curriculum that aims to empower students of color must acknowledge the history of their exclusion. Failure to acknowledge the biases of the dominant culture results in painful experiences for marginalized students such as that poignantly described by Foor, Walden, and Trytten (2007) for one female multi-minority socioeconomically disadvantaged engineering student. The exclusionary history for African Americans has been described by Slaton (2010), Lewis (2003), and Mutegi (2011). The history of exclusion for Latinos/as, compared with African Americans, is similar in the ways that society racializes, marks, and discriminates; it is also different because of the unique colonial and migratory histories that impact educational opportunities not least of which include questions of citizenship and language. It is important to consider broad social factors so that recruitment efforts do not unintentionally reproduce the status quo or fail because of unrecognized structural problems. For too long, the focus of recruitment and intervention efforts has been on changing the incoming students rather than on changing the existing structure of engineering.

From a gendered lens, for women in engineering, a critical aspect of exclusion emerges from popular stereotypes about the biological differences between the sexes with regard to competencies needed for STEM fields. Focusing on innate biological differences leads to the danger of providing an excuse for maintaining the status quo and inaction. Instead, educators should work to help all students learn needed skills. In a comprehensive review of the existing literature, Halpern, Benbow, Geary, Gur, Hyde, and Gernsbacher illuminate the complexity of the issues surrounding sex differences and underscore the importance of looking beyond biology to many other social factors including "the effects of family, neighborhood, peer, and school influences; training and experience; and cultural practices. . . . There are no single or simple answers to the complex questions about sex differences in science and mathematics" (2007, p. 1). For example, one particular sex difference that is often cited in engineering is that males are better at spatial skills (multi-views, rotation of objects, cross-section of solids) than females. Popular perceptions often inflate the importance and magnitude of this difference. In fact, research shows that the male advantage in this area, whether learned or not, is at the upper end of the ability distribution, and only includes a small segment of the population (Halpern et al., 2007). More importantly, research has shown that these spatial skills can be taught (Sorby, 2009; Sorby & Baartmans, 2000). Sheryl Sorby, a professor of mechanical engineering at Michigan Tech, and her colleagues developed a class in spatial visualizing skills for students who failed a preliminary test in this area. They demonstrated a dramatic increase in female engineering student retention (from 48% to 77%) for those who took the course. Spatial skills are but one example. Although gendered stereotypes abound in society, educators have the potential to create change if they transcend societal biases.

Curricular Reformation

While innovative efforts at pedagogical reform are gaining ground in engineering, reforming the content itself has received far less attention. We assert that such a reformation must occur if engineering is to undergo a process of desegregation. Creative energy is needed to move beyond the status quo, however, such change is controversial, contentious, and uncomfortable. How should engineering curricula evolve? Can faculty move beyond what is essentially "academic hazing" or the idea that painful experiences need to be repeated because "that is how I did it as a student" and examine what content is needed in courses today?

A creative example of successful curriculum restructuring that resulted in increased retention is the Wright State University (WSU) Model for Engineering Mathematics Education (Klingbeil, Mercer, Rattan, Raymer, & Reynolds, 2004; Klingbeil et al., 2008; Rattan & Klingbeil, 2013; WSU Model for Engineering Mathematics Education, n.d.). Faced with an alarmingly low retention rate, engineering faculty identified calculus as a big stumbling block because a high percentage of their students were not ready to take calculus at matriculation. Rather than trying to reform the calculus course, the researchers decided to offer their own course, EGR 101 Introductory Mathematics for Engineering Applications. Engineering programs offering focused math courses is not new. What is novel here is that students still needed to take the calculus course in the Math Department; however, it no longer served as a gateway course. The prerequisite course for physics and sophomore level engineering courses became the new engineering math course, EGR 101. This gave students the opportunity to take real engineering courses to determine if engineering was a good fit for them. Calculus was still required but could be taken later in the academic trajectory. Perhaps the most interesting aspect of this project is the content of the engineering math course. Nathan Klingbeil and colleagues developed the content by talking to faculty who taught the sophomore engineering courses and asking them what math (calculus and below) topics they actually used in their courses and for examples from their courses where the math is used. Then, these examples, with the identification of which sophomore course they are from, became the engineering math course. Thus, this project reshaped the curriculum by challenging the traditional prerequisites and allowed engineering faculty to revisit what math topics are used rather than just a laundry list of topics students should be exposed to. Although successful at this institution, application at others has faced challenges including disciplinary territorialism and broader resistance to change. Where else in the engineering curriculum would benefit from such a fresh look at the content?

Even more radical changes may be necessary to reform engineering education. This involves self-reflection by engineering educators and could expand to questioning the engineering "canon." As one of our engineering professors in one of our studies explains,

> [E]ngineers, when they sit down to teach a course or write a textbook, are writing what they were taught. And so there's something, there's a precedence effect where you are just sort of doing what was taught because that's what it is and because we don't talk about the canon in engineering. . . . Every other discipline talks about . . . "What are the classic texts? What are the key things that you need to know?" Even though we have accreditation and we have . . . some discussions about what constitutes a good engineer, it's very skill-focused. And we haven't really asked some of the questions that we should be asking. What do engineers need to know now? What do we need to know in order to plan the future? And to recognize that the choices that we are making

have an impact on what kinds of technology are going to be available in twenty years. (Lord & Camacho, 2007b)

This quote raises questions such as: Is there an engineering canon? If so, is it negotiable? Who decides and who should participate in this decision-making process? This extends into fields such as ethics and philosophy of engineering. What significant differences would appear in engineering curricula if these questions were considered? For example, an innovative text on thermodynamics and 21st-century energy problems offers a fresh look at a standard course in the engineering curriculum (Riley, 2012). Funded by the NSF, Jarosz and Busch-Vishniac conducted a national survey to examine the canon in mechanical engineering (2006) and later work resulting from this grant includes several novel textbooks featuring real-life examples in mechanics of solids, dynamics, thermodynamics, and fluid mechanics (see www. engineeringexamples.org/real_life_examples.htm). Considering curricular questions in light of the recognition of the gendered and racialized nature of engineering could lead to new breakthroughs.

COMMUNITY COLLEGE PATHWAYS

For Latinas and Latinos, interventions to encourage and support engineering must consider community colleges, since they "are the chief points of entry for Hispanic students who go to college" (Hagedorn & Lester, 2006). Studies show that over 44% of Latinos ages 18–24 enrolled in college attended community colleges, more than their White or Black counterparts (Fry, 2002). For older Latinos, the percentage is even higher, and the average age of Latinos in college is higher than for other groups (Fry, 2002). Some of the advantages of community colleges include low tuition, more evening classes to help students who work full-time, programs designed to accommodate part-time students, and English-as-a-second-language programs: "The strong commitment to work and family does not stop Latinos from enrolling, even part-time, but it may help explain why so few enroll full-time" (Fry, 2002, p. 6). Given the large number of Latinos/as who enter engineering through the community college pathway, their unique experiences merit further discussion and research. These institutions could potentially play a key role in advancing Latinos and Latinas in engineering, particularly for low-income students who may benefit from taking prerequisite classes at community colleges.

Enrolling in a community college is not a guarantee of transferring to a four-year institution. Researchers have shown that rates of four-year college graduation are less for students who start in community college than those for students who matriculate directly into four-year institutions (Fry, 2002). The pathways from two-year to four-year institutions for Latinos/as are often difficult, with few students successfully making the transition (Suarez, 2003). In 2008, only 25.7% of full-time Latino students at two-year colleges graduated in three years or less. This lagged behind Asians at 31.5% and Whites at 28.5% (Lee et al., 2011). Measurement of transfer rates is complicated and transfer readiness may be a more useful metric. Hagedorn and Lester (2006) analyzed 5,000 students and described "success" as passing the courses needed to permit transferring to a four-year institution. Among all Latino students, they found that Latinas did better than Latinos but found no significant differences in success by age or native language. After an average of six semesters, only 8.9% were "transfer ready." About one-third had made progress by passing at least one module. The mathematics modules proved particularly problematic. This has significant implications for engineering, which requires proficiency in mathematics and is related to the K–12 mathematics situation.

Suarez investigated the factors that contributed to Latino students transferring from two-year to four-year colleges (2003). She conducted interviews with students, counselors, and administrators. Her findings echo themes we have seen earlier in this chapter. She grouped these factors into three categories: individual, institutional, and environmental. Individual factors included personal drive, rigorous academic preparation, and education/career goals. Institutional factors included validation by staff and faculty, role models, institutional flexibility, thinking of transfer as a shared responsibility, and active minority student support programs. Environmental factors included the availability and assistance with financial aid, geographic proximity of the transfer university and the existence of a strong support system.

Many of the two-year institutions where Latinos go are HSIs (Perrakis & Hagedorn, 2010). In fact, 53% of HSIs are two-year institutions. HSIs have been shown to promote success for Latino students with 40% of all Latino associate's degree recipients coming from HSIs. Laden (2004) estimates that HSIs grant 37% of all Latino bachelor's degrees. Perrakis and Hagedorn (2010) investigated the experiences of students at an HSI community college in Los Angeles. They found that none of the students were aware of the institution's identity as an HSI. Eight of the ten Latino students interviewed said they were planning to transfer to a four-year institution. All but one said they wanted to stay close to home, family, and Latino culture. Several students emphasized the importance of being at an institution where there were a significant number of Latino students. One student describes her choice this way:

> I want to go to UCLA because it is close to my family and my friends and it is less White than some places. Like I could not go to Kansas or Missouri or maybe some other state that I think is really White. I mean I picked UCLA because it is Hispanic a bit and it is a really good school and I can get a good

education and be somebody. It is about getting it all, close to home, family, friends, and a good education. (Perrakis & Hagedorn, 2010, p. 804)

As we saw in Chapter 3, geography plays a significant role in the institutions that graduate engineering students. O'Connor (2010) showed that geography plays an important role for Latino community college enrollment. In a study using the National Education Longitudinal Study of 1988 (NELS:88) data set, she showed that Latino students who aspired to a bachelor's degree were more likely to enroll in community college than their Black or White counterparts. However, Latinos who lived in states with high Latino populations, specifically New York, Texas, Florida, and California, were more likely to go directly to a four-year college than a two-year college compared with White or Black students. She suggests that this may be linked to the preference of Latino students to live at home, along with the higher availability of community colleges outside these four states. The desire to stay at home was stronger for immigrants. However, generation in the United States did not have a significant effect on likelihood to attend a four-year institution. O'Connor stresses the importance of considering the impact of geography on student trajectories: "The intersections of geography and race, such as the one presented here between Hispanic origin and SHS (strong Hispanic states), can provide us with a unique understanding about the higher education paths of different student populations" (2010, p. 830). Because Latinos are not a monolithic group, and because Hispanic-serving institutions serve different populations that vary geographically, a more nuanced analysis that explores variation by Latino ethnic group is necessary to inform the development of specific and effective engineering recruitment strategies. Interventions designed to increase the number of Latinos in engineering education may have the best results if these efforts are targeted at HSIs, with special consideration in states with the largest populations.

ACADEMIC PREPARATION, ESPECIALLY IN MATH/SCIENCE

Creative efforts at the K–12 level are also needed to improve curricular offerings and innovative pedagogy to attract Latinos to engineering. Good examples of national academic programs aimed at precollege engineering include Project Lead the Way (www.pltw.org/), Try Engineering (www.tryengineering.org/), and Engineering Go For It (www.egfi-k12.org/). The most successful programs in K–12 offer hands-on, practical learning opportunities. Experiences with Lego robots have been shown to particularly help Latinos/as as well as girls of all races gain confidence and perform careful analysis before problem solving (Karp & Schneider, 2011). Without such projects there are no systematic opportunities within existing educational

structures that allow for experience with pre-engineering skills before college.

Since engineering has such significant math prerequisites, it is crucial that
students succeed in math in high school. First-generation students, which
include many Latinos, are less likely to take calculus in high school (Harrell
& Forney, 2003). Latino students continue to have lower SAT scores than
other groups: "Hispanic students should be encouraged, advised, and shown
the relevancy of completing rigorous academic coursework" (Harrell & Forney, 2003, pp. 148–149) particularly in math. Adopting creative approaches
for teaching math such as a "culturally relevant pedagogy" (Ladson-Billings
1994; 1995)—that is, a style of teaching that empowers students by incorporating relevant referents to their everyday lives—could have a dramatic impact in attracting them to the field of engineering. If students in K–12 see the
importance of learning math to their lives, it helps their performance in math
classes (Gutstein, Lipman, Hernandez, & de los Reyes, 1997; Hancock &
Yu, 2009), and enables more students to continue taking advanced math
classes so that they are in a position to make a choice about engineering,
rather than having a hollow choice of being interested but unprepared and
thus stunted (Torres-Ayala, 2009). Such a pedagogical approach requires an
investment in teacher development to equip them with the tools to diversify
their techniques in the classroom.

Finally, we recommend peer-mentoring programs to strengthen community alliances. In this model, college students earn credits for tutoring high
school youth; similarly, high school students earn community service hours
for working with their younger peers. Such a structural approach provides
ample opportunities for one-on-one attention; it allows for greater visibility
of the importance of math; it creates leadership opportunities at local levels
and generates a spirit of collaboration and role modeling.

OUTREACH EFFORTS

Engineering is stereotyped as antisocial and an unusual career for women
(c.f. Tonso, 2007). To stir girls' interests, it is critical to counter these stereotypes. The National Academy of Engineering's report *Changing the Conversation* (2008) encourages the engineering community to find creative new
ways of appealing to the next generation and girls in particular with taglines
such as "engineers make a world of difference" rather than "engineers work
hard" or "engineers are good at math and science." The engineering community could learn lessons from the medical community, which does not stress
its prerequisites such as "Be a Doctor, Take Organic Chemistry, and Stay Up
All Night," but rather the outcomes and impact of the work "Be a Doctor,
Save Lives." Specific marketing aimed at Latinas is needed. These efforts

need to be pluralistic, as in the United States Latinas are increasingly multi-cultural and represent hybrid identities. In elementary school, flashcards and textbook stories featuring career options can feature Latinas as engineers. There is a need for more social media sites and YouTube programming to highlight diversified careers with greater representation of Latinas. There are many well-respected role models in the Latino community that can be tapped for public marketing campaigns aimed at targeting Latino youth. As television programming increasingly features Latina actors in nonstereotypical roles (as upwardly mobile working women and not simply as hot Latin lovers or service-workers), their roles can be diversified to popularize representations of Latinas as engineers.

Some programs to recruit young people are very effective with certain populations but do not appeal to all. There are some programs that are wildly popular with boys, and are failing to attract a wide array of girls. For example, national competitions such as FIRST (For Inspiration and Recognition of Science and Technology) Robotics whose vision is "to transform our culture by creating a world where science and technology are celebrated *and* where young people dream of becoming science and technology leaders" (www.usfirst.org) and FIRST Lego League (www.firstlegoleague.org) should be careful of perpetuating notions of who belongs in engineering and narrow definitions of engineering. These programs are strong on promoting teamwork, problem solving, and gracious professionalism among young people. They have had a large national impact, excited many young people about robotics, and raised the profile of STEM education in the media. High costs for entry restrict access, however, and the highly competitive nature of the activities may inadvertently appeal more to boys in our culture and suggest that engineering necessarily means competition. Given the demographics of engineering, most of those volunteering as mentors are White males, most of whom are dedicated volunteers doing a great job. But what sorts of messages are sent to young people about who is excited about these activities if the leaders are all White men? This is a classic structural example of the masculine aspect of engineering embedded in extracurricular activities. What would these programs look like if they were designed specifically for an audience of all young girls? Answers to such questions rely on incorporating additional perspectives and bringing in a diversified pool of talent to generate more interest from girls. One solution might be to have interdisciplinary perspectives involved in designing the objectives and activities for these projects. Moreover, Latina students need to share in the excitement and learn from peers who have already participated in the projects. The inanimate constructions and productions need a social life. Our youth today are arguably more technologically literate than any previous generation. Moreover, their addictions to social media can be exploited for generating interest in new engineering-oriented activities. The endeavors of extracurricular engineering projects need to be reassessed with a different pool of potential participants in mind. Complexity and customization may be more appealing than embracing stereotypes of what girls are interested in or extreme focus on competition or warlike games. Although Milgram asserts that the color pink may be attractive to girls and women given cultural constructions and should therefore be central in marketing engineering to women (2011), such efforts should not be limited and segregated (such as pink Legos and jewelry for girls and space shuttles with moving parts for boys). Since playing with toys such as Legos has been linked to improving spatial, mathematical, and fine motors skills, it is problematic that such toys appeal primarily to boys. Recently, Lego has conducted extensive research to design their new line of products aimed at girls, Lego Friends:

> Lego confirmed that girls favor role-play, but they also love to build—just not the same way as boys. Whereas boys tend to be "linear"—building rapidly, even against the clock, to finish a kit so it looks just like what's on the box— girls prefer "stops along the way," and to begin storytelling and rearranging. Lego has bagged the pieces in Lego Friends boxes so that girls can begin playing various scenarios without finishing the whole model. (Wieners, 2011)

Those designing such toys acknowledge the sociological complexity of this task:

> The Lego Friends team is aware of the paradox at the heart of its work: To break down old stereotypes about how girls play, it risks reinforcing others. "If it takes color-coding or ponies and hairdressers to get girls playing with Lego, I'll put up with it, at least for now, because it's just so good for little girls' brains," says Lise Eliot. A neuroscientist at the Rosalind Franklin University of Medicine and Science in Chicago, Eliot is the author of *Pink Brain Blue Brain*, a 2009 survey of hundreds of scientific papers on gender differences in children. "Especially on television, the advertising explicitly shows who should be playing with a toy, and kids pick up on those cues," Eliot says. "There is no reason to think Lego is more intrinsically appealing to boys." (Wieners, 2011)

And yet, so often television advertising cognitively inscribes who should be building and designing projects and who should be taking care of babies, baking cupcakes, or playing with makeup and hair. While there is no reason to think Lego is more intrinsically appealing to boys, Lego brand has differentiated its product line to segment its market. This bifurcation is not without social effects; parents and gift-buyers assume the products are gender specific and, because of the rigidity of gender constructions in our society, crossing artificially constructed gender boundaries is socially taboo.

Programs designed primarily by women for girls to increase interest in STEM do exist. In addition to focusing on girls, two of these successful outreach efforts involve family members, which may be powerful for appealing to Latinas by broadening awareness of engineering practices, particularly if offered in Spanish and English. The "My Daughter Is an Engineer" program at California State University, Long Beach (CSULB), was designed by the Women in Engineering Outreach program under the leadership of two Asian female mechanical engineering professors. This innovative three-day residential program has mother-daughter teams participate in engineering-related activities together: "The program activities highlight topics on engineering in everyday life, academic success skills, and STEM-related hands-on projects. This program successfully attracted a high percentage of sixth-grade Latinas" (California State University Long Beach, 2012). One of the authors, Susan Lord, has been a workshop presenter at another excellent program, Expanding Your Horizons, whose mission is to encourage young women to pursue careers in STEM:

> Through Expanding Your Horizons (EYH) Network programs, we provide STEM role models and hands-on activities for middle and high school girls. Our ultimate goal is to motivate girls to become innovative and creative thinkers ready to meet 21st Century challenges. (Expanding Your Horizons Network, 2012)

The EYH Network has grown from a volunteer group of women scientists and educators in California in 1974 to a nationwide organization that received the 2010 National Science Board Award for Public Service. In 2009, EYH conferences attracted 32% minorities among their over 20,000 attendees (EYH, 2009). An important feature of EYH conferences is that separate programs for parents are offered along with the workshops for the girls. This is particularly helpful for families where transportation is an issue. For Latinas it is especially respectful to include family in educational efforts. This gives parents opportunities to learn more about applying to college, financing college, and STEM.

The field of engineering needs to be demystified so that young people can connect it to their experience of life and see the potential that it has to help people and provide an interesting career. Images in the larger society and popular culture need to be analyzed. The stereotypical "Computer Engineering Barbie" (clad in hot pink, holding a laptop, tiny waist, and toes poised for high-heels), works with narrow imagery of gender codes, for example, to appeal to the same market segment. *Engineer Your Life* brochures offer a different vision of engineering highlighting women and nontraditional types of engineering (www.engineeryourlife.org). The IEEE *Women in Engineering* (WIE) magazine also offers progressive visions in its advertisements (seewww.ieee.org/membership_services/membership/women/index.html).

An interesting example of an effort that has resulted in attracting a large number of women is Franklin W. Olin College of Engineering, which has over 40% women (Gibbons, 2010). Olin is a unique environment. It is a relatively new (opened in 2002), small (less than 400 students) college that only offers engineering undergraduate degrees. It focuses on creativity, passion, and enterprise (www.olin.edu). They require students to have a "passionate pursuit," making it acceptable to have other interests instead of devaluing or delegitimizing anything other than engineering. By privileging and honoring unique skill sets beyond the narrow technical, they achieved some of the highest percentages of women in the United States.

SOCIAL SUPPORT, NETWORKING, AND MENTORS

Research on Latino/a persistence in college has shown the importance of social support, including friends, family, and mentors. The support of friends and family were both found to have positive effects on the psychological adjustment of Latino/a college students (Rodriguez, Mira, Myers, Morris, & Cardoza, 2003). Interestingly, friend support was slightly more important. Family support has been shown to be important for Mexican American women (Garza, 1998). Mentoring, including student and faculty mentors, has been found to be particularly important for Latinos/as in college in several studies (Gloria, 1997; Gloria, Castellanos, Lopez, & Rosales, 2005; Torres & Hernandez, 2009–2010; Torres Campos et al., 2009). According to Bordes-Edgar, Arredondo, Kurpius, and Rund (2011), the most important predictors of academic persistence from first semester to four and a half years later were self-beliefs and mentoring. Compared to the Latino/a (mostly Mexican American) students who had not graduated, graduates had "stronger high school GPAs, more mentoring, and more positive initial academic persistence decisions" (2011, p. 358). In this study, no differences were found based on whether the mentor was also a Latino/a. Social support from friends on campus was important when the students were in their first year but did not predict their success four and a half years later, while perceived mentoring did. Although this study did not consider the academic major of the students, it is one of the few to point to longitudinal performance of Latino/a college students. Bordes-Edgar et al. argue that "the importance of social support and college GPA on student success should be disseminated to faculty working with students at all levels, not just freshmen, as a way to create a culture of success in classrooms and on campus for Latina/o students" (2011, p. 366). They advocate for more specific studies of the experiences of Latinas/os in college.

Faculty role models and mentors are essential for Latino/a student success in higher education (Cejda & Rhodes, 2004; Gándara, 1995; Perez Huber,

Huidor, Malagòn, Sánchez, & Solórzano, 2006). College mentoring and support was found to be a significant difference between retained and nonretained Latino engineering students (Lara, 2011). Hagedorn, Chi, Cepeda, and McClain (2007) found that Latino students had higher grades and course completions on campuses with a higher representation of Latino faculty. Latino faculty as role models may be particularly useful for Latino/a students, since their parents are the least likely of any group to have college educations (Harrell & Forney, 2003) and thus lack the experience to "help their children negotiate the demands and bureaucracies of college life" (Perrakis & Hagedorn, 2010, p. 799). As shown in Chapter 3, however, Latinos are seriously underrepresented in the ranks of higher education and engineering faculty, comprising only about 3% of full-time instructional faculty. A significantly larger percentage of faculty at HSIs are Latino, with estimates ranging from 13% for all HSIs to 60% at some institutions. Such high percentages enhance the chances that Latino students will find "culturally familiar, sensitive, and relatable role models and allies" (Perrakis & Hagendorn, 2010, p. 799). Faculty of color have been found to be more likely than White faculty to provide support and encouragement and raise Latino students' aspirations (Laden, 1999; Perrakis & Hagedorn, 2010; Turner & Myers, 2000). This may be a result of a heightened awareness by faculty of color of the challenges students of color face. However, given the predominance of White faculty in academia, it is critical that they be involved in mentoring of Latino students. Role models are also important in promoting the transfer of Latinos from community colleges to four-year institutions. In interviews with Latino community college students, Suarez found that

> [c]ounselors, students, faculty, and administrators served as important role models for students, especially, if they were of Hispanic descent. Students told me that it was important for them to be able to identify with someone on the campus (counselors, faculty, staff, administrators) who had shared similar experiences, whether academic or personal, and had succeeded. The knowledge that they were not the first to encounter and overcome adversity provided a certain degree of comfort and security. Administrators and counselors, in particular, stressed that when students saw other students who looked like them, who had similar experiences, and who had successfully transferred to MSU, then they too began to see their own opportunities for success. When students had an opportunity to see other Latino students succeed, their level of self-confidence was significantly strengthened. (2003, p.113)

Participating in social networks that provide a sense of community to students is also critical to academic persistence (Camacho & Lord, 2013). Research shows that groups such as the Society of Mexican American Engineers and Scientists (MAES), Society of Hispanic Professional Engineers (SHPE), National Society of Black Engineers (NSBE), and Society of Women Engineers (SWE), among others, help develop a culture of inclusivity in engineering education that leads to more opportunities for collective learning, contributing to social capital, sharing of experiences, and abetting feelings that students are not isolated (Brown, Flick, & Williamson, 2005; Frizell & Nave, 2008). Both SHPE and MAES began in the mid-1970s with the mission to support, encourage, and mentor Latino students in their undergraduate and professional engineering pursuits. Today these organizations continue to support Latino students and have expanded to connect students online through networking applications such as Facebook and Twitter. Grassroots organizations, support networks, and informal collectives (sometimes called *charlas* or *platicas* (meaning "chats"), that are student driven, can also be influential in promoting persistence. HSIs are also particularly well positioned to help Latino students sustain involvement with beneficial social networks that help Latinos succeed in college.

Finally, mentors guide student success, contribute to persistence, provide a template for professionalization in the field, and are influential in leading students to prestigious positions in industry or to pursue higher degrees (Aguirre, 2009; Chesler & Chesler, 2002; Sorkin, ReVelle, Beiderman, & Tingling, 2007; Wasburn, 2008). The ubiquity of resources widely available via the Internet allows mentoring and social support to transcend time and space via the virtual world. For example, the Minorities in Engineering Division (MIND) of the American Society for Engineering Education (ASEE) developed the MIND Links project, which gathers links to resources for studying and staying in engineering (Larrondo-Petrie & Esparragoza, 2012). This is updated yearly and organizes many resources for students, parents, professionals, academics, and administrators. In 2005, MIND Links had about 300 links; by 2012 it had grown to over 850. These include some resources specifically targeted at Latinos such as the Advancing Hispanics' Excellence in Technology, Engineering, Math, and Science (AHETEMS) program (http://shpe.tamu.edu/node/17) sponsored by SHPE. Latino and Latina engineers as role models negate public perceptions of stereotypes, can serve to provide leadership affecting policy at a macro level, and can inspire students at a micro level. The NSF actively recruits Latino mentors for their Role Models in Engineering webpage (www.nsf.gov/news/special_reports/profiles/). SHPE awards inspirational role models the STAR award for excellence in the field. The Hispanic Engineer National Achievement Award Corporation (HENAAC) honors

> highly accomplished STEM professionals who have achieved both academic and professional success in their respective fields. The purpose of the HE-NAAC Award nomination process is to highlight and honor these Hispanic success stories and provide this emerging and still largely untapped segment of our great nation's population access to these role models in order to motivate

more students to pursue degrees and careers in science, technology, engineering and math. (Great Minds in STEM, 2012)

Articles in the public media that highlight Latinas in STEM fields can be powerful and show the importance of these successful women's mentors and participation in outreach experiences in their youth and later as leaders giving back to the community (*El Sol de Cleveland*, 2011; Escalera & Romano, 2010). Similar efforts require broad publicity to capture the attention of Latino youth. As students increase their technological communication capacities through online networking, the visibility of role models will be enhanced with potential for greater impact.

PRESTIGE, MEANING, AND THE SOCIAL CONSTRUCTION OF AN *INGENIERO*

In addition to the structural issues discussed earlier, it is also important to consider symbolic factors. What it means to be an engineer in the Latino community translates into a unique social configuration and can provide a nuanced opportunity to target Latino youth because of the social prestige of engineering. This esteemed social status is manifested discursively as engineers are addressed with a different title in Spanish. The social title "*ingeniero*" is prestigious, socially comparable to being addressed as "doctor." This prestige attracts some Latinas to major in engineering. For example, in a study of Latina engineering majors at the University of Puerto Rico–Mayaguez, researchers found that the second and fifth most commonly cited reasons for deciding to study engineering were "engineering viewed as empowering career" and "prestigious career" (Cruz-Pol & Colom-Ustáriz, 2002). Parents and relatives also play an important role and were listed third. Such influences should be considered when appealing to Latinas.

Leaders in the engineering community need to diversify their promotion techniques to capture the interest of young students and entice them to want to "engineer" the future through technological innovation and design. Recent work in "changing the [engineering] conversation" needs to be more directly aimed toward Latino communities (National Academy of Engineering, 2008). For example, in describing the cultural aspects within engineering, researchers have identified the discursive power of labels ascribed to engineers such as "geek" or "nerd" or social outcast (Godfrey, 2007; Tonso, 2006). Such stigma, however, is less likely to be an obstacle for Latinos because of the high cultural status ascribed to engineering in Latino communities. A greater obstacle is the social isolation of being one of few Latino engineering students. Supportive networks are critical to attracting and retaining Latino engineering students. For Latinos in particular, these networks must engage community leaders, parents, and even grandparents who are often instrumental in familial decision making at the household level. Community "crosswalks" within higher education are particularly important for Latino college access (Oliva, 2008).

While engineering may be a path out of the working class into higher socioeconomic status, it can also lead more Latinos into the military. Even the Reserve Officers Training Corps (ROTC) program that strongly encourages students to pursue engineering majors in college also promotes a career in military leadership, which may have narrow, complex, and potentially dangerous opportunities for applying engineering skills. The Navy requirements for NROTC scholarships now mandate 85% of students in NROTC to study engineering or technical majors (U.S. Navy, 2010). The military underpinnings of engineering are deep and problematic (Hacker, 1989; Riley, 2008). Nonetheless, many Latinos are currently in the military as enlisted personnel (Pew Hispanic Center, 2003). The NSF recognizes that veterans leaving the military may provide a source of talent to address shortages in the engineering workforce and has funded projects to develop models for helping veterans make the transition from active duty to successful student (Lord et al., 2011). Future qualitative research is needed to explore the pathways of Latinos and Latinas drawn to the military and familial perceptions about how this relates to ideas about social class status, job prospects, and prestige.

CONCLUSION

In this chapter, we assert the need for a new vision of engineering education. If the endeavor of changing engineering will benefit all of society, then all societal actors need to be part of this process. Change is always difficult. Institutional and national support is critical for sustained engagement as we collectively work on these reformative efforts. As part of this process, we must engage conversations of structural inequities and support opportunity structures to reform the status quo. While academic units are invested in protecting territorial boundaries and resources, can we reach beyond our biases and disciplinary borders to re-envision what is needed for an educated person in the postmodern world?

Chapter Six

Conclusions

At the same time that these regrettable events [such as the 9/11 tragedy] were shaking the American ethos and national identity in the middle of the struggle against terrorism, new statistics were registering the increasing presence of . . . Latino scientists and engineers surfacing in corporate, governmental, and university laboratories as well as science and engineering departments of Ivy League and state universities. . . . What these two contrasting trends might represent for the future of the Latino community certainly has to be analyzed closely.

—Frank Bonilla and José Villegas (2003, pp. 209–210)

While popular ideas about retention in STEM (science, technology, engineering, math) suggest that women and minorities are at the greatest risk for dropping out or switching majors, recent data show that Latinos and Latinas who matriculate into engineering persist at the same rates as their White male counterparts (Lord et al., 2009). As we have reviewed in this book, what is surprising about this finding is that this persistence occurs in the face of tremendous odds. In Chapter 2, we characterized the context of engineering education as an exclusionary culture. Roughly 80% of all bachelor's degrees awarded in engineering are to men. The landscape of engineering education emerges from a strict curricular history, one influenced by the military-industrial complex. The hegemonic masculine character of engineering education continues to influence the climate internally; the canonical rigidity of the discipline seems to repel women and underrepresented minorities rather than attract them in higher education. Nonetheless, data from the Bureau of Labor Statistics indicate that engineering jobs continue to grow, and there continues to be a need for educated engineers to fill these gaps. The National Academy of Sciences asserts that the United States is challenged to maintain its position of global leadership: "Maintaining that vast and complex enterprise during an age of competition and globalization is challenging, but it is essential to the future of the United States" (National Academy of Sciences, National Academy of Engineering, & Institute of Medicine of the National Academies, 2007, p. 43).

Although some engineering needs can be filled with a global workforce, there is still a need for onsite engineers in the United States. Thus, there has been increasing alarm that the nation will not meet its own needs in reproducing a new generation of engineering leaders. This has been called a "crisis" particularly because the United States is failing to recruit increasing numbers of people into engineering education (Jackson, 2004b; Congressional Commission on the Advancement of Women and Minorities in Science, Engineering and Technology Development, 2000). Given that technology and society co-construct each other, it is imperative to have many diverse perspectives driving the innovative forces that produce new technologies. Without this, unacceptable failures such as the tragic errors caused by using adult male bodies as the standards for airbags, and racist technologies such as the so-called Ghetto App, will continue to occur.

Data from Chapter 3 illustrated that Latinas who matriculate into engineering are high achieving and successful in engineering education. We demonstrated that Latinas are also drawn to specific subdisciplines within engineering more than their male counterparts, namely civil and industrial. The problem continues to be that there are simply too few being recruited. Latinas who transfer into engineering have the highest graduation rates of any group in our data set. Latinas who persist in engineering programs surmount one of the last exclusionary and most segregated spaces remaining in academia today.

Using qualitative data as a case study, in Chapter 4 we examined how Latinas experience the climate in a top undergraduate engineering university. We organized their narratives using a framework called "microaggressions" to describe the obstacles they face. The women in our case study demonstrate steadfast persistence—they remain in the engineering major in spite of their encounters with these microaggressions. We provided insights into how they overcome and challenge these at a micro level. Their strategies comprise the "counterspaces" that they carve for themselves, and these include seeking out a social peer group that diverges from their male engineering counterparts. It also includes avoiding male-dominated study groups that discount their work, and seeking out professors for assistance rather than relying on peers. Latinas lament the sheer numbers of men in engineering that create false impressions that men are the smartest; they note that men are visibly the ones speaking up in class, creating the impression that they have all the answers and are the most knowledgeable. In our focus group, Latinas assert that such impressions stem from the lack of women and this perpetuates stereotypes that women engineers are inferior. Thus it is a circular problem—the lack of women in the field insidiously reinforces the assumption, even among women, that women are less capable. Because of stereotype threat, this can negatively affect how women perceive their performance, creating a context in which it is uncomfortable or intimidating to pose questions, provide solutions, and engage actively as leaders. These social forces exert a downward pressure on the potential for engineering to be transformed internally.

In Chapter 5, we reviewed and proposed strategies and practices that have the potential to diversify engineering. We re-envisioned engineering and proposed moving it from the borderlands into the core. Drawing on some of the best research in this area, we highlight innovative pedagogical strategies that yield more collaborative learning climates. In thinking about the content of standard engineering coursework and prerequisites, tremendous advancements remain to be seen that could influence and positively contribute to drawing in a broader population of students. More broadly, as a society, serious systemic problems affect Latinos in education; the community college pathway has been underutilized by engineering leaders to appeal to these students. Furthermore, administrators and faculty in Hispanic-serving institutions have the potential to play a pivotal role in changing the playing field for Latinos and Latinas who want to pursue engineering. Strengthening the community college pathway with special focus on Hispanic-serving institutions is an important area given the large number of Latinos and Latinas who follow this path. Appealing to the prestige and cultural capital associated with being an *ingeniero/ingeniera*, a high-status position among Latinos, might be powerful on a symbolic level.

Efforts to diversify engineering in higher education will fail if they do not extend into K–12 and adopt creative strategies for appealing to girls. Sexist beliefs continue to subtly influence how girls are socialized, and the media popularizes ideals about women's behaviors and interests. Few representations of women engineers circulate in popular media; by contrast, viewers are flooded with representations of objectified women. Future research is needed to understand how media representations of women push them away from science and engineering by reinscribing gendered norms. Where men are taught that their masculine responsibilities involve building and creating to the exclusion of domestic and nurturing skill sets, women are taught that self-objectification and achieving beauty standards take precedence over technical skills (deemed masculine). Too few representations of women suggest that women have the potential and capacity to build, create, contribute, transform, and engineer our social worlds. It is paradoxical that engineering leaders decry the need for more women to join the field of engineering when there are so few mechanisms in place to attract women and even fewer that value them for feminine perspectives within it. Strategies might include using variation in the extracurricular options available to girls in K–12, novel applications for teaching girls about engineering design, pedagogical changes in how engineering and math are taught, and circulating empowering representations of women engineer role models.

Our objectives in writing this book included illuminating invisible forms of power and privilege within engineering education and examining how these influence the borderlands of education. Latinas intersect multiple borderlands and thus provide a powerful perspective for exploring structural problems within the discipline of engineering. By disaggregating engineering from the larger STEM category and considering the unique case of Latinos and Latinas, we offered strategies for reimagining engineering and potentially reaching Latino youth. In this concluding chapter, we highlight larger societal problems that work against Latinos and how these intersect with the potential for Latinas in engineering education. We argue that our society needs the best minds, a diverse student body, and an influx of imaginative ideas so we can continue to work toward a peaceful, socially just, and productive society. Finally, we provide promising directions for research in engineering education.

SOCIAL LANDSCAPE OF LATINOS AND THE LATINO ENGINEERING PARADOX

Engineering, a field that has shaped the world's industrial and technological base, is ripe for an influx of Latino undergraduate students. Why do so few college-bound Latinos and Latinas choose engineering? There is a paradox for Latinos in engineering education. This "Latino Engineering Paradox" is a dialectical tension between (1) the call by federal leaders to diversify the field of engineering with Latino talent and (2) exclusionary anti-Latino rhetoric in current societal policies.

Based on quantitative measures alone, among all underrepresented minorities, Latinos are poised to have the greatest impact on the field of engineering. Latinos are currently America's largest minority population and are on the demographic fast track, suggesting the potential to create a more representative workforce in engineering, with Latinos helping to close the gap. As we have argued throughout the book, given that the vast majority of engineering students are White, recruiting more Latinos and Latinas would significantly broaden participation in engineering. Because of the shortage of engineers and the value of a variety of life experiences for enhancing innovation, leaders are asserting the need for greater diversity in engineering education and inviting Latinos and Latinas to the table.

As the quote at the beginning of this chapter suggests, contemporary social issues complicate the demand for, and meanings of, engineers. Prominent engineering publications highlight the importance of developing new technologies to address homeland security and the role of engineering innovations in preventing terrorist threats. Juan Lucena (2005) offers an insightful critique of the role of government policies since the 1940s in shaping the issues and language surrounding national threats and engineering priorities. Less research has examined the dialectical tensions embedded in the call for a more diverse engineering workforce. Engineering leaders seek to find technical solutions that protect the nation from external threats. The ideas of these threats, however, emerge in a charged sociocultural context, heavily influenced by a racialized history in which Latinos occupy a subaltern status because of political and economic conditions including conquest, colonialism, and immigration.

Structural Barriers Work against Latinas

The Latino educational pipeline is congested by a myriad of factors affecting their educational success (c.f. Chapa & De La Rosa, 2006). According to education experts, optimistic projections of demographics do not take into account the important qualitative variables that affect Latinos' participation in education as a whole including health care, nutrition, adequacy and stability of housing, parents' education, housing segregation, neighborhood environments, family income, access to preschool, and few engineering role models in minority communities (Gándara, 2006; Gándara & Contreras 2009; Rochin & Mello, 2007; Suárez-Orozco & Páez, 2002; Walsh, 1998). Although Latinos continue to make strides in educational attainment, the educational gap between Latinos and other groups continues to widen (Johnson, 2007). As MacDonald, Botti, and Clark assert, "the Latino narrative has been marked by a dialectic of educational access and societal constraint, of opportunity achieved and expectations tempered" (2007, p. 474).

Within schools, several ideological forces carve everyday social relations for Latino students. Gándara and Contreras theorize a persistent problem, the "politics of ethnicity and achievement"—suggesting that who deserves to be educated is a point of political contention (2009). At a micro level, "ethnoracial" tensions and divisions between White and Latino students in high school affect perceptions of Latino students' capabilities and potential. "Students who are visibly Latino are associated with inferior academic success" (Nunn, 2011, p. 1245). Angela Valenzuela (1999) argues in her compelling monograph *Subtractive Schooling* that part of the problem rests with high schools that structurally "subtract" from Latino students, divesting them of their language and culture. Many Latino students attend segregated schools where they find themselves concentrated among the most understaffed and under-resourced schools in the country where teachers experience high turnover and students feel that teachers are indifferent about their academic success (Valenzuela, 1999). These types of structural inequalities are among the factors that lead Latinos away from pursuing higher education. By contrast, schools with strong administrators, excellent teachers devoted to dismantling stereotypes (Ochoa, 2007), and good mentoring programs with effective role models (c.f. Aguirre, 2009) are those that channel Latinos toward the pipeline of success.

Sociopolitical Context and Racism against All Latinos and Latinas

Ideologies of meritocracy and politics of citizenship, in addition to low public school resources, complicate the social reproduction of Latinos. Politicians often respond to public outcries in ways that produce, echo, and perpetuate stereotypes, thereby legitimizing institutional racism. Many governmental policies, particularly in U.S.-Mexico border states, have sought to place limits on social services including education for both U.S.-born children of undocumented migrant workers (Chavez, 1994, 2008; Perea, 1996) and immigrant children (Contreras, 2009; Gonzales & Chavez, 2012). The widespread feelings of xenophobia and racism, arguably, are targeted toward all Latinos regardless of residency or citizenship status. Popular media representations position Latinos as second-class citizens, as outsiders, as social "Others" constructing imagery of Latinos as a risk to our nation (Chavez, 2001).

Because of the negative publicity associated with problems of immigration, and the social meanings associated with these politics of exclusion, many Latinos experience a blurring of national belonging; they are outside of the "imagined community" (Anderson, 1991; Chavez, 1994). Ideologies of nativism and xenophobia are related to ethnocentric borderland politics and the methods used to keep "the Other" out (Sánchez, 2011). For example, the goal of the post-9/11 Department of Homeland Security "Secure Border Initiative" is to "remove criminal aliens, immigration fugitives and other immigration violators from this country" (Department of Homeland Security, 2006). Analysts of the border theorize that the spectacles of deportations and militarization of the border are less about deterring illegal crossings and more about recrafting the political image of safety (Andreas, 2009).

One of the most damaging stereotypes that negatively affect all Latinos in education, both immigrant and nonimmigrant, is the perception of undocumented Latino workers and their children as "criminal aliens." This stereotype is compounded by the "criminalization of the classroom" in many urban areas, where disproportionately poor Black and Latino students are subjected to police searches and confrontations by police personnel on school campuses (Mukherjee, 2007). Nativists construct the demographic surge of Latinos in the United States as a national problem, reconstructing ideologies of who belongs, who has a right to succeed in this country, and who does not. Latinos are a heterogeneous group, yet the media constructs them as a monolith. The discourse of the "Latino threat" in schools and communities negates the rich contributions that Latinos make and ignores the social history that created a large Hispanic population in the United States (Chavez, 2008; Murillo, 2001). Public stereotypes, nativism, and xenophobic media imagery contribute to racialized policies that curtail resources into ethnic communities with severe effects on the education of children in low-income Latino communities.

Within this context, the pipeline for Latinos in engineering is clearly clogged. The pool of Latinos is demographically rich with potential; however, Latinos face a paradox in engineering education. While leaders in the engineering community seek to recruit a diverse population and draw in a wider pool of students, at the societal level, another set of voices systematically devalues and discriminates against the Latino population. Beyond the obstacles that exist within the educational pipeline, the pathway into engineering in particular has historically been a complex terrain marred by exclusionary forces. Recognizing the Latino paradox in engineering education is the first step toward social action. Engineers concerned with social justice can work toward empowering underrepresented students, diversifying the profession through interventions at a micro level, and proposing policy applications such as the ones described in Chapter 5. More research is needed to understand the problems and potential of all underrepresented populations in engineering to continue to make progress toward greater social justice.

Increasingly, engineers are effectuating change through social action. Brilliant scholars in the field are theorizing broader issues of social justice in engineering. *Engineering and Social Justice: In the University and Beyond*, edited by Caroline Baillie, Alice Pawley, and Donna Riley (2012), brings together insights from many scholars who are doing important pioneering work in this area. The authors in this book collectively provide some self-reflection on the social motives of engineers, critical analysis of how messages are received by diverse audiences, and insights into how engineering practice sets limiting boundaries in multiple ways. At an individual level, there are increasing numbers of influential leaders who work zealously to contribute to a different vision of engineering. It is worth mentioning the contributions of a few of these change-makers. Bevlee Watford, professor of industrial engineering, associate dean, and director of the Center for the Enhancement of Engineering Diversity at Virginia Tech University, has been working passionately for years, reaching out to underrepresented students and establishing policies and structures to promote their recruitment and retention. At the national level, in 2011, Watford became the first African American woman to chair the revitalized American Society for Engineering Education (ASEE) Diversity Committee (Watford, 2011). Leah Jamieson, professor of electrical and computer engineering, dean of engineering at Purdue University, and past president of IEEE (the International Society for Electrical Engineers), was instrumental in the IEEE's campaign to increase public visibility of engineering and the work on *Changing the Conversation*

(National Academy of Engineering, 2008) as well as cutting-edge work in service learning in engineering education (IEEE Global History Network, n.d.). Diana I. Centeno-Gomez, a native of Puerto Rico, an aerospace engineer at NASA, works on projects for the space shuttle ranging from software to biofuels. She is also an ardent community activist working with LATINA, Inc., a nonprofit volunteer group of Latina professional women, and groups that reach out to youth and victims of domestic violence (*El Sol de Cleveland*, 2011). There are also noteworthy organizations making strides to integrate transnational academic efforts in engineering education including the Latin American and Caribbean Consortium of Engineering Institutions (LACCEI), Engineering for the Americas (EftA), the Ibero American Science and Technology Education Consortium (ISTEC), and the International Federation of Engineering Education Societies (IFEES) (www.laccei.org/; http://efta.oas.org/english/cpo_sobre.asp; www.istec.org/; www.sefi.be/ifees/).

A valuable strategy for engineers is to reach across disciplines for inspiration and support. Physicists and computer scientists share similar problems as engineers, with abysmally low numbers of women and underrepresented minorities (Lord, 2010). Coalitions can be developed among these exclusivist fields, with experts from outside these disciplines providing synergistic ideas for applied work and community outreach. The insider/outsider perspectives discussed in Chapter 1 can provide valuable insights into the social dynamics of a disciplinary culture. In professions where the labor market is heavily segmented by gender, charismatic leaders are needed to reach across the field and build consensus. In this way, the borderlands of education can be transformed into fertile regions of critical thinking with a plurality of perspectives germinating and contributing to new growth. Reflecting on many social movements of the past, the most successful ones join forces to establish greater influence and enfranchise the marginal. Alliances need to be forged among groups such as the Society of Hispanic Professional Engineers (SHPE), National Action Council for Minorities in Engineering (NACME), Women in Engineering Programs and Advocates Network (WEPAN), Society of Women Engineers (SWE), Society for Advancement of Chicanos and Native Americans in Science (SACNAS), American Association for the Advancement of Science (AAAS), and professional societies for engineering subdisciplines such as electrical engineering (IEEE), mechanical engineering (ASME), civil engineering (ASCE), and industrial engineering (IIE). Finally, more research is needed into the pathways of persisters in engineering education, with special emphasis on understanding the perspectives of underrepresented groups in the borderlands of education.

PATHWAYS OF CHANGE: LATINA
ENGINEERS IN THE FUTURE

For Latinas to persist in engineering they must negotiate a complicated social and cultural terrain in higher education. Engineering education has its own borders that few outsiders permeate. It is one of the last frontiers in education that has failed to diversify. Engineering leaders have decried the United States' failure to produce new engineering professionals. This tension is exacerbated by the need to "secure the homeland" against potential terrorist threats. While the former call highlights the importance of diversifying the field of engineering with new Latino talent, the latter is conflated with exclusionary policies, racialized rhetoric and anti-Latino popular sentiments. Social forces shape the failure to recruit diverse students, particularly Latinos and Latinas, who represent the largest demographic minority group potentially poised to have the strongest impact on the field of engineering education. This paradox of Latinos in engineering education requires complex, manifold solutions. The solutions involve more than creating multifaceted educational policies and practices. They require a reframing of the field of engineering itself. Many efforts to diversify engineering by drawing in more women and underrepresented minorities are underway; however, these noble efforts are handicapped for two reasons. First, failing to disaggregate "underrepresented minorities" prevents the development of targeted strategies that appeal to members of a single subgroup, such as Mexican Americans or Puerto Ricans. Second, because of the few role models within the Latino engineering community, recruitment efforts may be stymied, suggesting the need for more partnerships between professional societies and community leaders. Organizations such as the Mexican American Legal Defense and Educational Fund (MALDEF) and the League of United Latin American Citizens (LULAC) have long battled for Latino civil rights including working to bring greater diversity to various fields, especially politics. Applied to the crisis in engineering, their influential efforts could broaden participation and challenge the status quo in engineering education.

Many contemporary problems in our society require engineering to be part of the solution. The expertise of engineers is required in addressing large-scale problems such as distribution of clean water or affordable and renewable energy, as well as smaller-scale ones such as medical devices for diabetes or technological innovations for inner-city classrooms. This is why a plurality of voices, of women's voices, Latino voices, voices from the margins, in short, a polysemic approach is critical. The quality of solutions to deeply complicated and multidisciplinary problems is enhanced with greater participation. As the old guard in engineering retires, the power and promise of engineering education remains to be seen. We need the best minds, a diverse student body and an influx of imaginative and creative dreams so that we can continue to work toward a peaceful and productive society. Our hope is that this book represents one small step forward/*adelante*. *¡Si se puede!*

References

ABET. (2012a). Accreditation criteria. Retrieved December 6, 2011, from www.abet.org/uploadedFiles/Accreditation/Accreditation_Process/Accreditation_Documents/Current/eac-criteria-2012-2013.pdf

ABET. (2012b). Accredited programs. Retrieved February 18, 2012, from http://main.abet.org/aps/AccreditedProgramsDetails.aspx?OrganizationID=84

Adelman, C. (1998). *Women and men of the engineering path: A model for analyses of undergraduate careers*. Washington, DC: U.S. Department of Education.

Aguirre, J. (2009). Increasing Latino/a representation in math and science: An insider's look. *Harvard Educational Review, 79*(4), 697–704.

Alfred, L. J., Atkins, C., Lopez, M., Chavez, T., Avila, V., & Paolini, P. (2005). A science pipeline pathway for training underrepresented students in the biomedical sciences. *Journal of Women and Minorities in Science and Engineering, 11*(1), 45–60.

America COMPETES Act (America Creating Opportunities to Meaningfully Promote Excellence in Technology, Education, and Science Act). (2007). HR 2272, 110th Cong. Retrieved February 21, 2012, from www.govtrack.us/congress/bill.xpd?bill=h110-2272&tab=summary

American Anthropological Association (AAA). (1997). *Response to OMB Directive 15: Race and ethnic standards for federal statistics and administrative reporting*. Arlington, VA: AAA. Retrieved September 3, 2012, from www.aaanet.org/gvt/ombdraft.htm

American Council on Education (ACE). (2006). *Minorities in higher education: Twenty-second annual status report*. New York: American Council on Education.

Anderson, B. (1991). *Imagined communities: Reflections on the origin and spread of nationalism*. New York: Verso.

Andreas, P. (2009). *Border games: Policing the U.S.-Mexico divide* (2nd ed.). Ithaca, NY: Cornell University Press.

Antonio, A. L. (2001). The role of interracial interaction in the development of leadership skills and cultural knowledge and understanding. *Research in Higher Education, 42*(5), 593–617.

Antonio, A. L., Chang, M. J., Hakuta, K., Kenny, D. A., Levin, S., & Milem, J. F. (2004). Effects of racial diversity on complex thinking in college students. *Psychological Science, 15*(8), 507–510.

Anzaldúa, G. E. (2007). *Borderlands/La Frontera: The new Mestiza* (3rd ed.). San Francisco, CA: Aunt Lute Books.

ASEE. (2009). Degrees awarded and enrollment reports. *ASEE Engineering Data Management System*. Washington, DC: ASEE.

ASEE. (2012a). President's Council on Jobs and Competitiveness to host deans of engineering, announce new partnership with ASEE. Retrieved February 21, 2012, from www.asee.org/

papers-and-publications/news-and-surveys/news/press-releases/president-s-council-on-jobs-and-competitiveness-to-host-deans-of-engineering-announce-new-partnership-with-asee

ASEE. (2012b). A world class commitment. *ASEE Capital Shorts February 10, 2012*, Washington, DC: ASEE.

Baillie, C., Pawley, A., & Riley, D. (Eds.). (2012). *Engineering and social justice: In the university and beyond*. West Lafayette, IN: Purdue University Press.

Baryeh, E. A., Squire, P. J., & Mogotsi, M. (2001). Engineering education for women in Botswana. *Australasian Journal of Engineering Education, 9*(2), 163–172.

Beddoes, K. D. (2012). Feminist scholarship in engineering education: Challenges and tensions. *Engineering Studies, 4*(2), 1–28.

Beede, D., Julian, T., Langdon, D., McKittrick, G., Khan, B., & Doms, M. (2011). Women in STEM: A gender gap to innovation. ESA Issue Brief #4-11. Washington, DC: U. S. Department of Commerce, Economics and Statistics Administration. Retrieved February 21, 2012, from www.esa.doc.gov/sites/default/files/reports/documents/womeninstemagaptoinnovation8311.pdf

Bertha Benz Memorial Club e.V. (n.d.). Bertha Benz Memorial Route. Retrieved September 6, 2012, from www.bertha-benz.de/indexen.php?inhalt=home

Besterfield-Sacre, M., Moreno, M., Shuman, L. J., & Atman, C. J. (2001). Gender and ethnicity differences in freshmen engineering student attitudes: A cross-institutional study. *Journal of Engineering Education, 90*, 477–489.

Beutel, A. M., & Nelson, D. J. (2005). The gender and race-ethnicity of faculty in top science and engineering research departments. *Journal of Women and Minorities in Science and Engineering, 11*, 389–402.

Bijker, W. E. (2012). Do we live in water cultures? A methodological commentary. *Social Studies of Science, 42*(4), 624–626.

Bijker, W. E., & Law, J. (Eds.). (1994). *Shaping technology/building society: Studies in sociotechnical change*. Cambridge, MA: MIT Press.

Bilimoria, D., & Buch, K. K. (2010). Engendering faculty diversity through more effective search and recruitment. *Change, 42*(4), 27–32.

Bilimoria, D., Joy, S., & Liang, X. (2008). Breaking barriers and creating inclusiveness: Lessons of organizational transformation to women faculty in academic science and engineering. *Human Resource Management, 47*, 423–441.

Bix, A. (2004). From engineeresses to girl engineers to good engineers: A history of women's American engineering education. *National Women's Studies Association, 16*(1), 27–49.

Blank, R. (2011, September 12). New ideas to advance STEM education in the U.S. Speech given at Brookings Institute. Retrieved September 6, 2012, from www.brookings.edu/events/2011/0912_stem_education.aspx

Bonilla, F., & Villegas, J. (2003). Reflections on Latino research after 9/11. *Latino Studies, 1*(2), 208–210.

Bordes-Edgar, V., Arredondo, P., Kurpius, S. R., & Rund, J. (2011). A longitudinal analysis of Latina/o students' academic persistence. *Journal of Hispanic Higher Education, 10*(4), 358–368.

Bradley, K. (2000). The incorporation of women into higher education: paradoxical outcomes? *Sociology of Education, 73*(1), 1–18.

Brainard, J. (2008, October 10). Community colleges seen as source of engineers. *Chronicle of Higher Education, 55*(7), A1.

Brainard, S. G., Metz, S. S., & Gillmore, G. M. (2000). *WEPAN pilot climate survey. Exploring the environment for undergraduate engineering students*. Retrieved March 15, 2007, from the Women in Engineering Programs and Advocates Network Web site: www.wepan.org

Bransford, J., Vye, N., & Bateman, H. (2004). *Creating high-quality learning environments: Guidelines from research on how people learn*. Washington, DC: National Academy Press.

Brawner, C. E., Camacho, M. M., Lord, S. M., Long, R. A., & Ohland, M. W. (2012). Women in industrial engineering: Stereotypes, persistence, and perspectives. *Journal of Engineering Education, 101*(2), 288–318.

Brawner, C. E., Lord, S. M., & Ohland, M. W. (2011, June). Undergraduate women in chemical engineering: Exploring why they come. *Proceedings of the 2011 ASEE Annual Conference*, Vancouver, BC.

Brown, S., Flick, L. & Williamson, K. (2005, October). Social capital in engineering education. *Proceedings of the 2005 Frontiers in Education Conference*. Indianapolis, IN.

Bruce, R. V. (1990). *Bell: Alexander Bell and the conquest of solitude*. Ithaca, NY: Cornell University Press.

Bureau of Labor Statistics. (2007). *Occupational outlook handbook*, 2008–09 edition. Retrieved August 12, 2010, from www.bls.gov/oco/ocos027.htm

Bureau of Labor Statistics. (2011). *Occupational outlook handbook*, 2010–11 Edition. Retrieved February 21, 2012, from www.bls.gov/oco/

Busch-Vishniac, I., & Jarosz, J. (2004). Can diversity in the undergraduate engineering population be enhanced through curricular change? *Journal of Women and Minorities in Science and Engineering, 19*, 255–281.

Calderon, H., & Saldívar, J. D. (Eds.). (1991). *Criticism in the borderlands: Chicano literature, culture, and ideology*. Durham, NC: Duke University Press.

California State University Long Beach. (CSULB). (2012). My daughter is an engineer. *Women in Engineering Outreach Program*. Retrieved September 6, 2012, from www.csulbwomenengr.org/my-daughter-is-an-engineer

Camacho, M. M. (2004). Power and privilege: Community service learning in Tijuana. *Michigan Journal of Community Service Learning, 10*(3), 31–42.

Camacho, M. M., & Lord, S. M. (2011a, October). "Microaggressions" in engineering education: Climate for Asian, Latina, and White women. *Proceedings of the 2011 Frontiers in Education Conference*, Rapid City, SD.

Camacho, M. M., & Lord, S. M. (2011b). *Quebrando fronteras:* Trends among Latino and Latina undergraduate engineers. *Journal of Hispanic Higher Education, 10*(2), 134–146.

Camacho, M. M., & Lord, S. M. (2013). Latinos and the exclusionary space of engineering education. *Latino Studies, 11*(1), 103–112.

Camacho, M. M., Lord, S. M., Brawner, C. E., & Ohland, M. W. (2010, October). Climate in undergraduate engineering education from 1995 to 2009. *Proceedings of the 2010 Frontiers in Education Conference*, Washington, DC.

Cantú, L. (2009). *The sexuality of migration: Border crossings and Mexican immigrant men.* N. A. Naples & S. Vidal-Ortiz (Eds.). New York: New York University Press.

Carlson, L., & Sullivan, J. (2004). Exploiting design to inspire interest in engineering across the K–16 engineering curriculum. *International Journal of Engineering Education, 20*(3), 372–378.

Caro, R. A. (1974). *The power broker: Robert Moses and the fall of New York.* New York: Random House.

Cech, E. A., & Waidzunas, T. J. (2011). Navigating the heteronormativity of engineering: The experiences of lesbian, gay, and bisexual students. *Engineering Studies, 3*(1), 1–24.

Cejda, B. D., Kaylor, A. J., & Rewey, K. L. (1998). Transfer shock in an academic discipline: The relationship between student majors and their academic performance. *Community College Review, 26*(3), 1–13.

Cejda, B., & Rhodes, J. H. (2004). Through the pipeline: The role of faculty in promoting associate degree completion among Hispanic students. *Community College Journal of Research and Practice, 28*(3), 249–262.

Chang, M. J. (2001). The positive educational effects of racial diversity on campus. In G. Orfield (Ed.), *Diversity challenged: Evidence on the impact of affirmative action* (pp. 175–186). Cambridge, MA: Harvard Education Publishing Group.

Chang, M. J. (2003). *Compelling interest: Examining the evidence on racial dynamics in colleges and universities*. Stanford, CA: Stanford University Press.

Chang, M. J., Denson, N., Saenz, V., & Misa, K. (2006). The educational benefits of sustaining cross-racial interaction among undergraduates. *Journal of Higher Education, 77*(3), 430–455.

Chapa, J., & De la Rosa, B. (2006). The problematic pipeline: Demographic trends and Latino participation in graduate science, technology, engineering, and mathematics programs. *Journal of Hispanic Higher Education, 5*(3), 203–221.

Chavez, L. R. (1994). The power of the imagined community: The settlement of undocumented Mexicans and Central Americans in the United States. *American Anthropologist, 96*(5), 52–73.

Chavez, L. R. (1998). *Shadowed lives: Undocumented immigrants in American society* (2nd ed.). Fort Worth, TX: Harcourt Brace College Publishers.

Chavez, L. R. (2001). *Covering immigration: Popular images and the politics of the nation.* Berkeley, CA: University of California Press.

Chavez, L. R. (2008). *The Latino threat: Constructing immigrants, citizens, and the nation.* Stanford, CA: Stanford University Press.

Chesler, N. C., & Chesler, M. A. (2002). Gender-informed mentoring strategies for women engineering scholars: On establishing a caring community. *Journal of Engineering Education, 91*(1), 49–55.

Chou, R., & Feagin, J. (2008). *The myth of the model minority: Asian Americans facing racism.* Boulder, CO: Paradigm Publishers.

Chronicle of Higher Education. (2008, September 5). Engineering and the liberal arts: Strangers no longer. *Chronicle of Higher Education, 55*(2), A76. Retrieved August 22, 2012, from http://chronicle.com/article/Engineeringthe-Liberal/11657

Cohoon, J. M., Nable, M., & Boucher, P. (2011, October). Conflicted identities and sexism in computing graduate programs. *Proceedings of the 2011 Frontiers in Education Conference,* Rapid City, SD.

Collins, P. H. (1986). Learning from the outsider within: The sociological significance of Black feminist thought. *Social Problems, 33*(6), S14–S32.

Collins, P. H. (1990). *Black feminist thought: Knowledge, consciousness, and the politics of empowerment.* New York: Routledge Press.

Collins, P. H. (2000). *Black feminist thought: Knowledge, consciousness, and the politics of empowerment* (2nd ed.). New York: Routledge Press.

Collins, P. H. (2006). *From Black power to hip hop: Racism, nationalism, and feminism.* Philadelphia, PA: Temple University Press.

Concannon, J. P., & Barrow, L. H. (2009). A cross-sectional study of engineering students' self-efficacy by gender, ethnicity, year and transfer status. *Journal of Science Education and Technology, 18*(3), 163–172.

Congressional Commission on the Advancement of Women and Minorities in Science, Engineering and Technology Development (CAWMSET). (2000). *Land of plenty: Diversity as America's edge in science, engineering and technology.* Washington, DC: Government Printing Office.

Contreras, F. (2009). *Sin papeles y rompiendo barreras*: Latino students and the challenges of persisting in college. *Harvard Educational Review, 74*(4), 560–586.

Cordero, R., DiTomaso, N., & Farris, G. F. (1997). Gender and race/ethnic composition of technical work groups: Relationship to creative productivity and morale. *Journal of Engineering and Technology Management, 13,* 205–221.

Coyle, E. J., Jamieson, L. H., & Oakes, W. C. (2005). EPICS: Engineering projects in community service. *International Journal of Engineering Education, 21*(1), 139–150.

Crenshaw, K. (1989). Demarginalizing the intersection of race and sex: A Black feminist critique of antidiscrimination doctrine, feminist theory and antiracist politics. *University of Chicago Legal Forum,* 139–167.

Crenshaw, K. (2011). Postscript. In H. Lutz, M. T. Herrera Vivar, & L. Supik (Eds.), *Framing intersectionality: Debates on a multi-faceted concept in gender studies* (pp. 221–234). Burlington, VT: Ashgate Publishing.

Cruz-Pol, S., & Colom-Ustáriz, J. (2002, June). A case study: High percentages of women in engineering college at UPRM. *Proceedings of the Women in Engineering Programs and Advocates Network (WEPAN) 2002 Conference,* San Juan, Puerto Rico.

Davidow, W. H. (2012). Our tools are using us: Human brains can't cope with today's technology. *IEEE Spectrum,* 51–56.

Davis, C.-S., & Rosser, S. (1996). Program and curricular interventions. In C.-S. Davis, A. B. Ginorio, C. S. Hollinshead, B. B. Lazarus, P. M. Rayman, & associates (Eds.), *The Equity Equation.* San Francisco, CA: Jossey-Bass.

Davis, I., DeLoatch, E., Kerns, S., Morell, L., Purdy, C., Smith, P., & Truesdale, S. (2006, June). Best practices for promoting diversity in graduate engineering education. *Proceedings of the 2006 ASEE Annual Conference*, Chicago, IL.

Davis, K. (2008). Intersectionality as buzzword: A sociology of science perspective on what makes a feminist theory successful. *Feminist Theory, 9*(1), 67–85.

Delgado Bernal, D., Alemán, E. Jr., & Garavito, A. (2009). Latina/o undergraduate students mentoring Latina/o elementary students: A borderlands analysis of shifting identities and first-year experiences. *Harvard Educational Review, 74*(4), 560–586.

Department of Homeland Security. (2006). *Department of Homeland Security Unveils Comprehensive Immigration Enforcement Strategy for the Nation's Interior.* Retrieved February 1, 2009, from www.dhs.gov/xnews/releases/press_release_0890.shtm

El Sol de Cleveland. (2011, September 7). Local Latina NASA engineer receives national recognition. Retrieved February 29, 2012, from http://www.elsoldecleveland.com/news/1404/local-latina-nasa-engineer-receives-national-recognition

Escalera, C., & Romano, G. (2010). The future in the STEM field. *Latina Style Magazine, 16* (5). Retrieved September 6, 2012, from http://latinastyle.com/magazine/features/67/the-future-in-the-stem-field/

Eschenbach, E. A., Cashman, E., Waller, A. A., & Lord, S. M. (2005, October). Incorporating feminist pedagogy into the engineering learning experience. *Proceedings of the 2005 Frontiers in Education Conference*, Indianapolis, IN.

Eschenbach, E. A., Lord, S. M., Camacho, M. M., & Cashman, E. (2012, October). Special session: Race and the idea of privilege in the engineering classroom. *Proceedings of the 2012 Frontiers in Education Conference*, Seattle, WA.

Esparragoza, I. E., Larrondo-Petrie, M. M., Jordan, R., & Saavedra, J. P. (2007, June). Forming the global engineer for the Americas: Global educational experiences and opportunities involving Latin America and the Caribbean. *Proceedings of the 2007 ASEE Annual Conference*, Honolulu, HI.

Espinosa, L. (2009). *Pipelines and pathways: Women of color in STEM majors and the experiences that shape their persistence* (Doctoral dissertation). University of California, Los Angeles, CA.

Etzkowitz, H., Kemelgor, C., Neuschatz, M., & Uzzi, B. (1994). Barriers to women in academic science and engineering. In W. Pearson Jr. and I. Fechter (Eds.), *Who will do science? Educating the next generation.* Baltimore, MD: Johns Hopkins University Press.

Etzkowitz H., Kemelgor, C., Neuschatz, M. Uzzi, B., & Alonzo. J. (1994). The paradox of critical mass for women in science. *Science, 266*, 51–54.

Expanding Your Horizons (EYH) Network. (2009). *EYH 2009 Annual Report.* Oakland, CA: Expanding Your Horizons Network. Retrieved September 6, 2012, from www.expandingyourhorizons.org/about/reports.php

Expanding Your Horizons (EYH) Network. (2012). An Introduction to EYH. Retrieved from www.expandingyourhorizons.org/about/mission.php

Farley, T. (2007). The cell-phone revolution. *American Heritage of Invention & Technology, 22* (3), 8–19.

Faulkner, W. (2000). Dualisms, hierarchies and gender in engineering. *Social Studies of Science, 30*(5), 759–792.

Faulkner, W. (2001). The technology question in feminism: A view from feminist technology studies. *Women's Studies International Forum, 24*(1), 79–95.

Faulkner, W. (2007). Nuts and bolts and people: Gender-troubled engineering identities. *Social Studies of Science, 37*(3), 331–356.

Frank, R., Akresh, I. R., & Lu, B. (2010). Latino immigrants and the U.S. racial order: How and where do they fit in? *American Sociological Review, 75*(3), 378–401.

Fines, B. G. (1997). Competition and the curve. *University of Missouri-Kansas City Law Review, 65*, 879.

Foor, C. E., & Walden, S. E. (2009). "Imaginary engineering" or "re-imagined engineering": Negotiating gendered identities in the borderland of a college of engineering. *NWSA Journal, 21*(2), 41–64.

Foor, C. E., Walden, S. E., & Trytten, D. A. (2007). "I wish that I belonged more in this whole engineering group": Achieving individual diversity. *Journal of Engineering Education, 96*(2), 103–115.

Frehill, L. M. (2004). The gendered construction of the engineering profession in the United States, 1893–1920. *Men and Masculinities, 6*(4), 383–403.

Frizell, S., & Nave, F. (2008, June). An investigation of factors affecting the persistence of African-American women in engineering degree programs. *Proceedings of the 2008 American Society for Engineering Education Conference*, Pittsburgh, PA.

Froyd, J. E., & Ohland, M. W. (2005). Integrated engineering curricula. *Journal of Engineering Education, 94*(1), 147–164.

Fry, R. (2002). *Latinos in higher education: Many enroll, too few graduate.* Washington, DC: Pew Hispanic Center.

Gándara, P. (1995). *Over the ivy walls: The educational mobility of low-income Chicanos.* Albany, NY: SUNY Press.

Gándara, P. (2006). Strengthening the academic pipeline leading to careers in math, science, and technology for Latino students. *Journal of Hispanic Higher Education, 5*(3), 222–237.

Gándara, P., & Contreras, F. (2009). *The Latino education crisis: The consequences of failed social policies.* Cambridge, MA: Harvard University.

Gándara, P., & Maxwell-Jolly, J. (1999, December). *Priming the pump: Strategies for increasing the achievement of underrepresented minority undergraduates.* New York: The College Board, chapter 4 and p. 28. Retrieved from www.collegeboard.org/research/html/PrimingThePump.pdf (item number 987257)

Garza, L. (1998). The influence of pre-college factors on the university experiences of Mexican American women. *Aztlán, 23*, 119–135.

Gibbons, M. T. (2002). Engineering on the rise. *ASEE profiles of engineering and engineering technology colleges*, 2002 edition. Washington, DC: ASEE.

Gibbons, M. T. (2008). Engineering by the numbers. *ASEE profiles of engineering and engineering technology colleges*, 2008 edition. Washington, DC: ASEE.

Gibbons, M. T. (2010). Engineering by the numbers. *ASEE profiles of engineering and engineering technology colleges*, 2010 edition. Washington, DC: ASEE. Retrieved February 17, 2012, from www.asee.org/papers-and-publications/publications/college-profiles

Glass, J. C. Jr., & Harrington, A. R. (2002). Academic performance of community college transfer students and "native" students at a large state university. *Community College Journal of Research and Practice, 26*, 415–430.

Gloria, A. M. (1997). Chicana academic persistence: Creating a university-based community. *Education and Urban Society, 30*, 107–121.

Gloria, A. M., Castellanos, J., Lopez, A. G., & Rosales, R. (2005). An examination of academic nonpersistence decisions of Latino undergraduates. *Hispanic Journal of Behavioral Sciences, 27*, 202–223.

Godfrey, E. (2007, June). Cultures within cultures: Welcoming or unwelcoming for women? *Proceedings of the 2007 ASEE Annual Conference*, Honolulu, HI.

Godfrey, E. G., & Parker, L. (2010). Mapping the cultural landscape in engineering education. *Journal of Engineering Education, 99*(1), 5–22.

Gonzales, P. M., Blanton, H., & Williams, K. J. (2002). The effects of stereotype threat and double-minority status on the test performance of Latino women. *Personality and Social Psychology Bulletin, 28*, 659–670.

Gonzales, R. G., & Chavez, L. R. (2012). "Awakening to a nightmare": Abjectivity and illegality in the lives of undocumented 1.5-generation Latino immigrants in the United States. *Current Anthropology, 53*(3), 255–281.

Graham, L. P. (2007). Profiles of persistence: A qualitative study of undergraduate women in engineering (Doctoral dissertation). Virginia Polytechnic Institute and State University. Retrieved December 7, 2011, from http://scholar.lib.vt.edu/theses/public/etd-45816 2539751141/etd.pdf

Great Minds in STEM. (2012). HENAAC awards. Retrieved from www.greatmindsinstem.org/henaac/awards/

Gurin, P., Dey, E. L., Hurtado, S., & Gurin, G. (2002). Diversity and higher education: Theory and impact on educational outcomes. *Harvard Educational Review, 72*(3), 330–366.

Gutstein, E., Lipman, P., Hernandez, P., & de los Reyes, R. (1997). Culturally relevant mathematics teaching in a Mexican American context. *Journal for Research in Mathematics Education, 28*(6), 709–737.

Hacker, S. (1989). *Pleasure, power, and technology: Some tales of gender, engineering, and the cooperative workplace.* Boston, MA: Unwin Hyman, Inc.

Hagedorn, L. S., Chi, W., Cependa, R. M., & McLain, M. (2007). An investigation of critical mass: The role of Latino representation in the success of urban community college students. *Research in Higher Education, 48*(1), 73–92.

Hagedorn, L. S., & Lester, J. (2006). Hispanic community college students and the transfer game: Strikes, misses, and grand slam experiences. *Community College Journal of Research and Practice, 30*, 827–853.

Halpern, D. F., Benbow, C. P., Geary, D. C., Gur, R. C., Hyde, J. S., & Gernsbacher, M. A. (2007). The science of sex differences in science and mathematics. *Psychological Science in the Public Interest, 8*(1), 1–51.

Hancock, C., & Yu, E. (2009, April). The impact of culturally relevant pedagogy on the academic achievement of multicultural students. *American Association for Educational Research (AERA) Annual Conference*, San Diego, CA.

Hanson, S. L. (1997). *Lost talent: Women in the sciences.* Philadelphia, PA: Temple University Press.

Haraway, D. J. (1987). A manifesto for cyborgs: Science, technology, and socialist feminism in the 1980s. *Australian Feminist Studies, 2*(4), 1–42.

Haraway, D. J. (1996). *Simians, cyborgs, and women: The reinvention of nature.* New York: Routledge.

Harrell, P. E., & Forney, W. S. (2003). Ready or not, here we come: Retaining Hispanic and first-generation students in postsecondary education. *Community College Journal of Research and Practice, 27*, 147–156.

Hartman, M., Hartman, H., & Kadlowec, J. (2007, June). Gender differences across engineering majors. *Proceedings of the 2007 ASEE Annual Conference*, Honolulu, HI.

Heller, J. D. (1972). *Letter report on federal expenditures to aid Cuban refugees.* Washington, DC: United States General Accounting Office. Retrieved September 6, 2012, from http://archive.gao.gov/f0902c/092404.pdf

Heller, P., & Hollabaugh, M. (1992). Teaching problem solving through cooperative grouping. Part 2: Designing problems and structuring groups. *American Journal of Physics, 60*, 637–644.

Heywood, J. (2012a, June). Engineering at the crossroads: Implications for educational policy makers. 2012 Distinguished Lecture. *Proceedings of the 2012 ASEE Annual Conference*, San Antonio, TX.

Heywood, J. (2012b, June). The response of higher and technological education to changing patterns of employment. *Proceedings of the 2012 ASEE Annual Conference*, San Antonio, TX.

Hill, C., Corbett, C., & St. Rose, A. (2010). *Why so few? Women in science, technology engineering, and mathematics.* Washington, DC: AAUW Press.

Hills, J. R. (1965). Transfer Shock: The academic performance of the junior college transfer. *Journal of Experimental Education, 33*(2), 201–215.

Hispanic Association of Colleges and Universities (HACU). (n.d.). *Member Hispanic-serving institutions (HSIs).* Retrieved September 6, 2012, from www.hacu.net/assnfe/CompanyDirectory.asp?STYLE=2&COMPANY_TYPE=1,5&SEARCH_TYPE=0

Hoffman, M., Richmond, J., Morrow, J., & Salomone, K. (2002). Investigating sense of belonging in first-year college students. *Journal of College Student Retention, 4*(3), 227–56.

Humes, K. R., Jones, N. A., & Ramirez, R. R. (2011). *Overview of race and Hispanic origin: 2010.* 2010 Census Briefs. C2010BR-02. Washington, DC: U.S. Census Bureau. Retrieved September 3, 2012, from www.census.gov/prod/cen2010/briefs/c2010br-02.pdf

Hurtado, S. (2001). Linking diversity and educational purpose: How diversity affects the classroom environment and student development. In G. Orfield (Ed.), *Diversity challenged: Evidence on the impact of affirmative action* (pp. 187–203). Cambridge, MA: Harvard Education Publishing Group.

Hurtado, S., & Carter, D. F. (1997). Effects of college transition and perceptions of the campus racial climate on Latino college students' sense of belonging. *Sociology of Education, 70*(1), 342–345.

IEEE Global History Network. (n.d.). *Leah Jameison.* Retrieved September 3, 2012, from www.ieeeghn.org/wiki/index.php/Leah_Jamieson

Jackson, S. A. (2004a). Appendix B: The beauty of diverse talent. In S. Malcolm, D. E. Chubin, & J. K. Jesse (Eds.), *Standing our ground: A guidebook for STEM educators in the post-Michigan era.* Washington, DC: American Association for the Advancement of Science. Retrieved September 6, 2012, from www.aaas.org/standingourground/

Jackson, S. A. (2004b). *The quiet crisis: Falling short in producing American scientific and technical talent.* Retrieved September 2, 2012, from www.bestworkforce.org/PDFdocs/Quiet_Crisis.pdf

Jarosz, J. P., & Busch-Vishniac, I. J. (2006). A topical analysis of mechanical engineering curricula. *Journal of Engineering Education, 95*, 241–248.

Johnson, A. (2007). Graduating underrepresented African American, Latino, and American Indian students in science. *Journal of Women and Minorities in Science and Engineering, 13*(1), 1–22.

Justin-Johnson, C. (2004). *Good fit or chilly climate: An exploration of the persistence experiences of African-American women graduates of predominantly White college science programs* (Unpublished doctoral dissertation). University of New Orleans, LA.

Kanter, R. M. (1977). *Men and women of the corporation.* New York: Basic Books.

Karp, T., & Schneider, A. (2011, October). Evaluation of a K–8 LEGO robotics program. *Proceedings of the 2011 Frontiers in Education Conference*, Rapid City, SD.

Kerr, K. H. (2006, November). *The experience of being a transfer student at a four-year university.* Paper presented at the Association for the Study of Higher Education. Garden Grove, CA. Retrieved December 7, 2011, from www.pathwaystocollege.net/pcnlibrary/ViewBiblio.aspx?aid=21667&backurl=%2Fpcnlibrary%2FUserSearch.aspx%3Fv%3DKeywords%26s%3D%2522NATN%2520Archive%2522

Keyes, A. (2012, January 25). This app was made for walking—but is it racist? *NPR All Things Considered.* Retrieved August 27, 2012, from www.npr.org/2012/01/25/145337346/this-app-was-made-for-walking-but-is-it-racist

Kilgore, D., Shepard, S., Atman, C. J., & Chachra, D. (2011, June). Motivation makes a difference, but is there a difference in motivation? *Proceedings of the 2011 ASEE Annual Conference*, Louisville, KY.

Kimmel, M. S. (2010). Introduction: Toward a pedagogy of the oppressor. In M. S. Kimmel & A. L. Ferber (Eds.), *Privilege: A Reader* (2nd ed.). Boulder, CO: Westview Press.

King, J. (2012, January 31). Why Microsoft's so-called "Avoid Ghetto" app is really American. *Colorlines.* Retrieved August 27, 2012, from http://colorlines.com/archives/2012/01/why_microsofts_so-called_avoid_ghetto_app_is_really_american.html

Kirchmeyer, C. (1993). Multicultural task groups: An account of the low contribution level of minorities. *Small Group Research, 24*(1), 127–148.

Klingbeil, N. W., Mercer, R. E., Rattan, K. S., Raymer, M. L., & Reynolds, D. B. (2004, June). Rethinking engineering mathematics education: A model for increased retention, motivation and success in engineering. *Proceedings of the 2004 ASEE Annual Conference*, Salt Lake City, UT.

Klingbeil, N. W., Rattan, K., Raymer, M., Reynolds, D., Mercer, R., Kukreti, A., & Randolph, B. (2008, June). The WSU model for engineering mathematics education: A multiyear assessment and expansion to collaborating institutions. *Proceedings of the 2008 ASEE Annual Conference*, Pittsburgh, PA.

Knight, D. W., Carlson, L. E., & Sullivan, J. F. (2003, June). Staying in engineering: Effects of a hands-on, team-based, first-year projects course on student retention. *Proceedings of American Society for Engineering Education Annual Conference*, Nashville, TN.

Laden, B. V. (1999). Celebratory socialization of culturally diverse students in academic programs and support services. In K. M. Shaw, J. R. Valadez, & R. A. Rhoads (Eds.), *Community colleges as cultural texts: Ethnographic explorations of organizational culture* (pp. 173–194). New York: SUNY Press.

Laden, B. V. (2001). Hispanic-serving institutions: Myths and realities. *Peabody Journal of Education, 76*(1), 73–92.

Laden, B. V. (2004). Hispanic-serving institutions: What are they? Where are they? In B. V. Laden (Ed.), Special issue on Hispanic-serving community colleges, *Community College Journal of Research and Practice, 28*(3), 181–198.

Ladson-Billings, G. (1994). *The Dreamkeepers: Successful teachers of African American children*. San Francisco, CA: Jossey-Bass.

Ladson-Billings, G. (1995). Toward a theory of culturally relevant pedagogy. *American Educational Research Journal, 32*(3), 465–491.

Lara, E. (2011). *Familial and cultural variables as predictors of retention of Latino engineering students* (Doctoral dissertation). University of Southern California.

Larrondo-Petrie, M. M., & Esparragoza, I. E. (2012, June). MIND LINKS 2012: Resources to motivate minorities to study and stay in engineering. *Proceedings of the 2012 ASEE Annual Conference*, San Antonio, TX.

Larrondo-Petrie, M. M., Otero Gephardt, Z., & Esparragoza, I. E. (2012, June). LACCEI initiatives for faculty leadership and development: Enhancing engineering program quality in the Americas and beyond. *Proceedings of the ASEE Inaugural International Forum*, San Antonio, TX.

Lattuca, L. R., Terenzini, P. T., & Volkwein, J. F. (2006). *Engineering change: A study of the impact of EC2000*. Baltimore, MD: ABET.

LeCompte, M. D. (1993). A framework for hearing silence: What does telling stories mean when we are supposed to be doing science? In D. McLaughlin & W. G. Tierney (Eds.), *Naming silenced lives: Personal narratives and process of educational change* (pp. 9–27). New York: Routledge.

Lee, J. M., Contreras, F., McGuire, K. M., Flores-Ragade, A., Rawls, A., Edwards, K., & Menson, R. (2011). *The college completion agenda 2011 progress report: Latino edition*. New York: College Board Advocacy and Policy Center. Retrieved December 7, 2011, from http://completionagenda.collegeboard.org/latino/

Lee, S. J. (2009). *Unraveling the "model minority" stereotype: Listening to Asian American youth* (2nd ed.). New York: Teachers College Record Press.

Le Espiritu, Yen. (1992). *Asian American panethnicity: Bridging institutions and identities*. Philadelphia, PA: Temple University Press.

Lewis, B. F. (2003). A critique of literature on the under-representation of African Americans in science: Directions for future research. *Journal of Women and Minorities in Science and Engineering, 9*(3–4), 361–373.

Library of Congress. (2010). Bill summary and status. 111th Congress, HR 5116. Retrieved February 21, 2012, from http://thomas.loc.gov/cgi-bin/bdquery/z?d111:H.R.5116

Locks, A. M., Hurtado, S., Bowman, N. A., & Oseguera, L. (2008). Extending notions of campus climate and diversity to students' transition to college. *Review of Higher Education, 31*(3), 257–285.

Lohan, M. (2000). Constructive tensions in feminist technology studies. *Social Studies of Science, 30*(6), 895–916.

Long, R.A. (2008). *MIDFIELD* (The Multiple-Institution Database for Investigating Engineering Longitudinal Development). Available from: https://engineering.purdue.edu/MIDFIELD

Lord, S. M. (2000). Service-learning in engineering at the University of San Diego: Thoughts on first implementation. In E. Tsang (Ed.), *Projects that matter: Concepts and models for service-learning in engineering*. Washington, DC: American Association for Higher Education.

Lord, S. M. (2010, March 16). Success in undergraduate engineering programs: A comparative analysis by race and gender (invited talk). *American Physical Society (APS) March Meeting*, Portland, OR.

Lord, S. M., & Camacho, M. M. (2007a, June). Why pedagogy matters: Faculty narratives. *Proceedings of the 2007 ASEE Annual Conference*, Honolulu, HI.

Lord, S. M., & Camacho, M. M. (2007b, October). Effective teaching practices: Preliminary analysis of engineering educators. *Proceedings of the 2007 Frontiers in Education Conference*, Milwaukee, WI.

Lord, S. M., Camacho, M. M., & Aneshansley, C. (2008, June). Applying "cultural consensus analysis" to a subgroup of engineering educators. *Proceedings of the 2008 ASEE Annual Conference*, Pittsburgh, PA.

Lord, S. M., Camacho, M. M., Layton, R. A., Long, R. A., Ohland, M. W., & Wasburn, M. H. (2009). Who's persisting in engineering? A comparative analysis of female and male Asian, Black, Hispanic, Native American, and White students. *Journal of Women and Minorities in Science and Engineering, 15*(2), 167–190.

Lord, S. M., Kramer, K. A., Olson, R. T., Kasarda, M., Hayhurst, D., Rajala, S., Green, R., & Soldan, D. L. (2011, October). Special session: Attracting and supporting military veterans in engineering programs. *Proceedings of the 2011 Frontiers in Education Conference*, Rapid City, SD.

Lord, S. M., Layton, R. A., & Ohland, M. W. (2011). Trajectories of electrical engineering and computer engineering students by race and gender, *IEEE Transactions on Education, 54*(4), 610–618.

Lucena, J. C. (2005). *Defending the nation: U.S. policymaking to create engineers and scientists from Sputnik to the "War against Terrorism."* Lanham, MD: University Press of America.

MacDonald, V.-M., Botti, J. M., & Clark, L. H. (2007). From visibility to autonomy: Latinos and higher education in the U.S., 1965–2005. *Harvard Educational Review, 77*(4), 474–504.

Madriz, E. (2003). Focus groups in feminist research. In N. K. Denzin & Y. S. Lincoln (Eds.), *Collecting and interpreting qualitative materials* (pp. 363–388). Thousand Oaks, CA: Sage.

Maestas, R., Vaquera, G. S., & Zehr, L. M. (2007). Factors impacting sense of belonging at a Hispanic-serving institution. *Journal of Hispanic Higher Education, 6*(3), 237–256.

Malcolm, S., Chubin, D. E., & Jesse, J. K. (2004). *Standing our ground: A guidebook for STEM educators in the post-Michigan era.* Washington, DC: American Association for the Advancement of Science.

Margolis, J., & Fisher, A. (2002). *Unlocking the clubhouse: Women in computing.* Cambridge, MA: MIT Press.

Maton, K. I., Hrabowski, F. A., & Schmitt, C. L. (2000). African American college students excelling in the sciences: College and postcollege outcomes in the Meyerhoff Scholars Program. *Journal of Research in Science Teaching, 37*(7), 629–654.

Mattis, C., & Sislin, J. (Eds.). (2005). *Enhancing the community college pathway to engineering careers.* Washington, DC: National Academies Press.

McIlwee, J., & Robinson, J. G. (1992). *Women in engineering: Gender, power, and workplace culture.* Albany, NY: SUNY Press.

McNair Scholars Program. (2012). Embrace his legacy. Create your own. *McNair Scholars Program: A U.S. Department of Education TRIO Program.* Retrieved February 18, 2012, from http://mcnairscholars.com/about/

Milgram, D. (2011). How to recruit women and girls to the science, technology, engineering, and math (STEM) classroom. *Technology and Engineering Teacher, 71*(3), 4–8.

Millett, C., & Nettles, M. (2006). Expanding and cultivating the Hispanic STEM doctoral workforce: Research on doctoral student experiences. *Journal of Hispanic Higher Education, 5*(3), 258–287.

Mills, C. Wright. (1959). *The sociological imagination.* Oxford: Oxford University Press.

Miyake, A., Kost-Smith, L. E., Finkelstein, N. D., Pollock, S. J., Cohen, G. L., & Ito, T. A. (2010). Reducing the gender achievement gap in college science: A classroom study of values affirmation. *Science, 30*, 1233.

Moser, I. (2006). Sociotechnical practices and difference: On the interferences between disability, gender, and class. *Science, Technology, & Human Values, 31*(5), 537–564.

Mukherjee, E. (2007). *Criminalizing the classroom: The over-policing of New York schools.* New York: ACLU Report. Retrieved September 6, 2012, from www.nyclu.org/pdfs/ criminalizing_the_classroom_report.pdf

Murillo, E. G., Jr. (2001). How does it feel to be a problem? "Disciplining" the transnational subject in the American South. In S. Wortham, E. Hamann, & E. G. Murillo Jr. (Eds.), *Education in the new Latino diaspora: Policy and the politics of identity.* Westport, CT: Ablex.

Mutegi, J. W. (2011). The inadequacies of "science for all" and the necessity and nature of a socially transformative curriculum approach for African American science education. *Journal of Research in Science Teaching, 48*, 301–316.

Naples, N. (2009, October 9–30). Borderlands studies and border theory: Linking activism and scholarship for social justice. *Compass Interdisciplinary Virtual Conference.* Retrieved August 31, 2012, from http://compassconference.files.wordpress.com/2009/10/civc-paper-borderlands-studies-and-border-theory-linking-activism-and-scholarship-for-social-justice-nancy-a-naples.pdf

Nash, J. C. (2008). Re-thinking intersectionality. *Feminist Review, 89*, 1–15.

National Academy of Engineering (NAE). (2008). *Changing the conversation: Messages for improving public understanding of engineering.* Retrieved February 16, 2012, from www. nap.edu/catalog.php?record_id=12187

National Academy of Engineering (NAE). (2009). *Greatest engineering achievements of the 20th century.* Retrieved February 14, 2009, from www.greatachievements.org

National Academy of Sciences, National Academy of Engineering, & Institute of Medicine of the National Academies. (2007). *Rising above the gathering storm: Energizing and employing America for a brighter economic future.* Washington, DC: National Academies Press. Retrieved from www.nap.edu/catalog/11463.html

National Action Council for Minorities in Engineering (NACME). (2008). *Confronting the "new" American dilemma, underrepresented minorities in engineering: A data-based look at diversity.* Retrieved July 26, 2008, from www.nacme.org/news/americandilemma.html.

National Center for Education Statistics (NCES). (2000). *Entry and persistence of women and minorities in college science and engineering education.* NCES 2000–601 (G. Huang, N. Taddese, & E. Walter. Project Officer: S. S. Peng). Washington, DC: Author, 2000. http:// nces.ed.gov/programs/digest/d08/tables/dt08_227.asp

National Center for Education Statistics (NCES). (2003). Table 254. Full-time and part-time faculty and instructional staff in degree-granting institutions, by race/ethnicity, sex, and selected characteristics. Retrieved February 29, 2012, from http://nces.ed.gov/programs/ digest/d09/tables/dt09_254.asp

National Center for Education Statistics (NCES). (2008). *Total fall enrollment in degree-granting institutions by race/ethnicity of student and type and control of institution: Selected years, 1976–2007.* Retrieved December 6, 2011, from http://nces.ed.gov/programs/digest/ d08/tables/dt08_227.asp

National Council for Research on Women. (2001). *Balancing the equation: Where are women and girls in science, engineering and technology?* New York: National Council for Research on Women.

National Research Council (NRC). (2006). To recruit and advance: Women students and faculty in science and engineering. *Report of the Committee on the Guide to Recruiting and Advancing Women Scientists and Engineers in Academia and the Committee on Women in Science and Engineering.* Washington, DC: National Academies Press.

National Research Council (NRC). (2011, July 19). Report offers new framework to guide K–12 science education, calls for shift in the way science is taught in U.S. *News from the National Academies.* Retrieved August 22, 2012, from www8.nationalacademies.org/ onpinews/newsitem.aspx?RecordID=13165

National Science Foundation (NSF). (2008a). Table 2-8. Intentions of freshmen to major in S& E fields, by race/ethnicity and sex: 2008. *Women, minorities, and persons with disabilities in science and engineering.* Retrieved February 17, 2012, from www.nsf.gov/statistics/wmpd/ pdf/tab2-8.pdf

National Science Foundation (NSF). (2008b). Table 5-4. Bachelor's degrees awarded to women, by field, citizenship, and race/ethnicity: 2000–08. *Women, minorities, and persons with disabilities in science and engineering.* Retrieved February 17, 2012, from www.nsf.gov/statistics/wmpd/pdf/tab5-4.pdf

National Science Foundation (NSF). (2008c). Table 5-5. Bachelor's degrees awarded to men, by field, citizenship, and race/ethnicity: 2000–08. *Women, minorities, and persons with disabilities in science and engineering.* Retrieved February 17, 2012, from www.nsf.gov/statistics/wmpd/pdf/tab5-5.pdf

National Science Foundation (NSF). (2008d). Table 5-7. Bachelor's degrees, by race/ethnicity, citizenship, sex, and field: 2008. *Women, minorities, and persons with disabilities in science and engineering.* Retrieved May 26, 2011, from www.nsf.gov/statistics/wmpd/pdf/tab5-7.pdf

National Science Foundation (NSF). (2008e). Table c-10. Bachelor's degrees awarded to U.S.-citizen and permanent-resident Hispanics, by institution type and field: 1994–2001. *Women, minorities, and persons with disabilities in science and engineering.* Retrieved January 19, 2010, from www.nsf.gov/statistics/wmpd/archives.cfm

National Science Foundation (NSF). (2009a). Table 5-7. Bachelor's degrees, by race/ethnicity, citizenship, sex, and field: 2009. *Women, minorities, and persons with disabilities in science and engineering.* Retrieved September 6, 2012, from www.nsf.gov/statistics/wmpd/pdf/tab5-7.pdf

National Science Foundation (NSF). (2009b). Table 5-9. Bachelor's degrees awarded by all institutions and HHEs to Hispanic U.S. citizens and permanent residents, by field: 2001–09. *Women, minorities, and persons with disabilities in science and engineering.* Retrieved February 17, 2012, from www.nsf.gov/statistics/wmpd/pdf/tab5-9.pdf

Nevarez, C. (2001). Mexican Americans and other Latinos in postsecondary education: Institutional influences. *ERIC Digest.* ED459038. Retrieved December 6, 2011, from www.ericdigests.org/2002-3/mexican.htm

Nosek, B. A., Banaji, M. R., & Greenwald, A. G. (2002). Math = male, me = female, therefore math ≠ me. *Journal of Personality and Social Psychology, 83*(1), 44–59.

Nosek, B. A., Smyth, F. L., Sriram, N., Lindner, N. M., Devos, T., Ayala, A., & Bar-Anan, Y. (2009). National differences in gender-science stereotypes predict national sex differences in science and math achievement. *Proceedings of the National Academy of Science, 106*(26), 10593–97.

Nunn, L. M. (2011). Classrooms as racialized spaces: Dynamics of collaboration, tension, and student attitudes in urban and suburban high schools. *Urban Education, 46*(6), 1226–1255.

Ochoa, G. L. (2007). *Learning from Latino teachers.* San Francisco, CA: Jossey-Bass.

O'Connor, N. (2010). Geography and Hispanic community college enrollment. *Community College Journal of Research and Practice, 34*, 814–832.

Ohland, M. W., Brawner, C. E., Camacho, M. M., Layton, R. A., Long, R. A., Lord, S. M., & Wasburn, M. H. (2011). Race, gender, and measures of success in engineering education. *Journal of Engineering Education, 100*(2), 225–252.

Ohland, M. W., Pomeranz, H. R., & Feinstein, H. W. (2006, June). The comprehensive assessment of team member effectiveness: A new peer evaluation instrument. *Proceedings of the 2007 ASEE Annual Conference*, Chicago, IL.

Ohland, M. W., Sheppard, S. D., Lichtenstein, G., Eris, O., Chachra, D., & Layton, R. A. (2008). Persistence, engagement, and migration in engineering. *Journal of Engineering Education, 97*(3), 259–278.

Oliva, M. (2008). Latino access to college: Actualizing the promise and potential of K–16 partnerships. *Journal of Hispanic Higher Education, 7*(2), 119–130.

Oliver, P., Marwell, G., & Teixeira, R. (1985). A theory of the critical mass: I. Interdependence, group heterogeneity, and the production of collective action. *American Journal of Sociology, 91*(3), 522–556.

Orfield, G., Losen, D., Wald, J., & Swanson, C. (2004). *Losing our future: How minority youth are being left behind by the graduation rate crisis.* Cambridge, MA: The Civil Rights Project at Harvard University.

Ortiz, F. I. (1986). Hispanic American women in higher education: A consideration of the socialization process. *Aztlán, 17*(2), 125–152.

Pappamihiel, N. E., & Moreno, M. (2011). Retaining Latino students: Culturally responsive instruction in colleges and universities. *Journal of Hispanic Higher Education, 10*(4), 331–344.

Pascarella, E., & Terenzini, P. (2005). *How college affects students: Vol. II. A third decade of research*. San Francisco, CA: Jossey-Bass.

Pawley, A. (n.d.). Research in feminist engineering (RIFE). Retrieved September 6, 2012, from http://feministengineering.org/

Pawley, A. L. (2007, June). Gendered boundaries: Using a "boundary" metaphor to understand faculty members' descriptions of engineering. *Proceedings of the 2007 Frontiers in Education Conference*, Milwaukee, WI.

Perea, J. F. (1996). *Immigrants out! The new nativism and the anti-immigrant impulse in the United States*. New York: NYU Press.

Pérez Huber, L., Huidor, O., Malagòn, M. C., Sánchez, G., & Solórzano, D. G. (2006). *Critical transitions in the Latina/o educational pipeline*. Report for the 2006 Latina/o Education Summit, Los Angeles, CA.

Perrakis, A., & Hagedorn, L. S. (2010). Latino/a student success in community colleges and Hispanic-serving institution status. *Community College Journal of Research and Practice, 34*, 797–813.

Pew Hispanic Center. (2003). *Hispanics in the military fact sheet*. Washington, DC: Pew Hispanic Center. Retrieved September 3, 2012, from http://pewhispanic.org/files/reports/17.pdf

Pham, M. (2011, September 28). California considers adopting new science standards for K–12. *Daily Sundial*, Retrieved August 9, 2012, from http://sundial.csun.edu/2011/09/california-considers-adopting-new-science-standards-for-k-12/

Phipps, A. (2007). Re-inscribing gender binaries: Deconstructing the dominant discourse around women's equality in science, engineering, and technology. *Sociological Review, 55*(4), 768–787.

Pierce, C. M. (1970). Offensive mechanisms. In F. B. Barbour (Ed.), *The black '70s* (pp. 265–282). Boston, MA: Porter Sargent.

Pierce, C. M. (1995). Stress analogs of racism and sexism: Terrorism, torture, and disaster. In C. V. Willie, P. P. Rieker, B. M. Kramer, & B. S. Brown (Eds.), *Mental health, racism, and sexism* (pp. 277–293). Pittsburgh, PA: University of Pittsburgh Press.

Poor, H. V. (2007, Spring). Engineering as a liberal art: Taking a broad view. *Eta Kappa Nu: The Bridge Magazine*.

Prince, M. (2004). Does active learning work? A review of the research. *Journal of Engineering Education, 93*(3), 223–231.

Prince, M., & Felder, R. M. (2006). Inductive teaching and learning methods: Definitions, comparisons, and research bases. *Journal of Engineering Education, 95*(2), 123–138.

Pritchard, S. B. (2011). *Confluence: The nature of technology and the remaking of the Rhône*. Cambridge, MA: Harvard University Press.

Purdy, C., DeLoatch, E., Kerns, S., Morell, L., et al. (2008, June). Implementing a multi-faceted approach for promoting diversity in graduate engineering education. *Proceedings of the 2008 ASEE Annual Conference*, Pittsburgh, PA.

Purdy, C., DeLoatch, E., Kerns, S., Morell, L., Smith, P., Truesdale, S., & Waugh, B. (2007, June). Articulating a multifaceted approach for promoting diversity in graduate engineering education. *Proceedings of the 2007 ASEE Annual Conference*, Honolulu, HI.

Rattan, K. S., & Klingbeil, N. W. (2013). *Introductory mathematics for engineering applications*. Hoboken, NJ: John Wiley & Sons.

Rhodes, R. (2011). *Hedy's folly: The life and breakthrough inventions of Hedy Lamarr, the most beautiful woman in the world*. New York: Doubleday Press.

Riley, D. (2003). Employing liberative pedagogies in engineering education. *Journal of Women and Minorities in Science and Engineering, 9*(2), 137–158.

Riley, D. (2012). *Engineering thermodynamics and 21st century energy problems: A textbook companion for student engagement*. San Rafael, CA: Morgan & Claypool.

Riley, D. M. (2008). *Engineering and social justice.* San Rafael, CA: Morgan and Claypool.

Riley, D. M., & Pawley, A. L. (2011, June). Complicating difference: Exploring and exploding three myths of gender and race in engineering education. *Proceedings of the 2011 ASEE Annual Conference,* Louisville, KY.

Roberts, H. (2012, January 18). Racist or realistic? Fears Microsoft "Avoid the Ghetto" app will damage economies of poor communities. *Daily Mail.* Retrieved August 27, 2012, from www.dailymail.co.uk/news/article-2088667/Critics-say-Microsoft-Avoid-Ghetto-app-dam age-economies-poor-communities.html#ixzz24mnvB1Ss

Rochin, R., & Mello, S., (2007). Latinos in science: Trends and opportunities. *Journal of Hispanic Higher Education, 6*(4), 305–355.

Rodriguez, N., Mira, C. B., Myers, H. F., Morris, J. K., & Cardoza, D. (2003). Family or friends: Who plays a greater supportive role for Latino college students? *Cultural Diversity and Ethnic Minority Psychology, 8,* 236–250.

Rosaldo, R. (1989). *Cultural and truth: The remaking of social analysis.* Boston, MA: Beacon Press.

Rosser, S. (1993). Female friendly science: Including women in curricular content and pedagogy in the sciences. *Journal of General Education, 42*(3), 190–220.

Rosser, S. (1998). Group work in science, engineering, and mathematics: Consequences of ignoring gender and race. *College Teaching, 46*(3), 82–88.

Rosser, S. V. (2012). *Breaking into the lab: Engineering progress for women in science.* New York: NYU Press.

Saenz, V. B., & Ponjuan, L. (2009). The vanishing Latino male in higher education. *Journal of Hispanic Higher Education, 8*(1), 54–89.

Sánchez, R. (2011). The toxic tonic: Narratives of xenophobia. *Latino Studies, 9*(1), 126–144.

Sandler, B. R., Silverberg, L. A., & Hall, R. M. (1996). *The chilly classroom climate: A guide to improve the education of women.* Washington, DC: National Association for Women in Education (NAWE).

Sanoff, A. P. (2005). Competing forces. *ASEE Prism.* Retrieved February 29, 2012, from www. prism-magazine.org/women/feature_competing.cfm

Santovec, M. (1999). Campus climate affects female engineering undergrads. *Women in Higher Education, 8*(7), 5.

Segura, D. A., & Zavella, P. (2008). Introduction: Gendered borderlands. *Gender & Society, 22*(5), 537–544.

Sevo, R. (2011). *Basics about disabilities and science and engineering education.* Published by Ruta Sevo. Available from www.lulu.com/spotlight/sevo

Seymour, E., & Hewitt, N. M., (1997). *Talking about leaving: Why undergraduates leave the sciences.* Boulder, CO: Westview Press.

Singletary, S. L., Ruggs, E. N., Hebl, M. R., & Davies, P. G. (2009). *Stereotype threat: Causes, effects, and remedies.* Retrieved September 6, 2012, from www.engr.psu.edu/awe/misc/ARPs/ARP_StereotypeThreat_Overview_31909.pdf

Slaton, A. E. (2010). *Race, rigor, and selectivity in U.S. engineering: The history of an occupational color line.* Cambridge, MA: Harvard University Press.

Slaton, A. E. (2011, June). Metrics of marginality: How studies of minority self-efficacy hide structural inequities. *Proceedings of the 2011 ASEE Annual Conference,* Louisville, KY.

Slaughter, J. B., & McPhail, I. P. (2007). New demands in engineering, science and technology. *Black Collegian, 38*(1), 31–35.

Smith, D., Turner, C. S. V., Osei-Kofi, N., & Richards, S. (2004). Interrupting the usual: Successful strategies for diverse faculty. *Journal of Higher Education, 75*(2), 133–160.

Smith, K., Sheppard, S., Johnson, D., & Johnson, R. (2005). Pedagogies of engagement: Classroom-based practices. *Journal of Engineering Education, 94*(1), 87–101.

Smith, R., DiTomaso, N., Farris, G., & Cordero, R. (2001). Favoritism, bias, and error in performance ratings of scientists and engineers: The effects of power, status, and numbers. *Sex Roles, 45*(5–6), 337–358.

Solórzano, D. G., Ceja, M., & Yosso, T. J. (2000). Critical race theory, racial microaggressions, and campus racial climate: The experiences of African American college students. *Journal of Negro Education, 69*(1–2), 60–73.

Sonnert, G., Fox, M. F., & Adkins, K. (2007). Undergraduate women in science and engineering: Effects of faculty, fields, and institutions over time. *Social Science Quarterly, 88*(5), 1333–1356.

Sorby, S. A. (2009). Educational research in developing 3-D spatial skills for engineering students. *International Journal of Science Education, 31*(3), 459–480.

Sorby, S. A., & Baartmans, B. J. (2000). The development and assessment of a course for enhancing the 3-D spatial visualization skills of first year engineering students. *Journal of Engineering Education, 89*(3), 301–307.

Sorkin, S., ReVelle, P., Beiderman, A., & Tingling, T. (2007, September). Interventions to promote degree completion in science, technology, engineering, and mathematics. *International Conference on Engineering Education*, Coimbra, Portugal.

Sosnowski, N. H. (2002). *Women of color staking a claim for cyber domain: Unpacking the racial/gender gap in science, mathematics, engineering and technology (SMET)* (Unpublished doctoral dissertation). University of Massachusetts, Amherst.

Stake, R. E. (1995). *The art of case study research.* Thousand Oaks, CA: Sage.

Steele, C. M. (1997). A threat in the air: How stereotypes shape the intellectual identities and performance. *American Psychologist, 52*, 613–629.

Steele, C. M., Spencer, S. J., & Aronson, J. (2002). Contending with group image: The psychology of stereotype and social identity threat. In M. Zanna (Ed.), *Advances in experimental social psychology* (vol. 34, pp. 379–440). New York: Academic Press.

Stevens, R., Amos, D., Garrison, L., & Jocuns, A. (2007, June). Engineering as lifestyle and a meritocracy of difficulty: Two pervasive beliefs among engineering students and their possible effects. *Proceedings 2007 ASEE Annual Conference,* Honolulu, HI.

Suarez, A. L. (2003). Forward transfer: Strengthening the educational pipeline for Latino community college students. *Community College Journal of Research and Practice, 27*, 95–117.

Suárez-Orozco, M., & Páez, M. (Eds.). (2002). *Latinos: Remaking America.* Berkeley, CA: University of California Press and the David Rockefeller Center for Latin American Studies at Harvard University.

Sue, D. W. (2010). *Microaggressions in everyday life: Race, gender, and sexual orientation.* Hoboken, NJ: John Wiley & Sons.

Sue, D. W., Capodilupo, C. M., Torino, G. C., Bucceri, J. M., Holder, A. M. B., Nadal, K. L., & Esquilin, M. (2007). Racial microaggressions in everyday life: Implications for clinical practice. *American Psychologist, 62*(4), 271–286.

Tate, E. D., & Linn, M. C. (2005). How does identity shape the experiences of women of color engineering students? *Journal of Science Education and Technology, 14*(5–6), 483–493.

Tillberg, H. K., & Cohoon, J. M. (2005). Attracting women to the CS major. *Frontiers, 26*(1), 126–140.

Tonso, K. L. (2006). Student engineers and engineer identity: Campus engineer identities as figured world. *Cultural Studies of Science Education, 1*(2), 1871–1502.

Tonso, K. L. (2007). *On the outskirts of engineering: Learning identity, gender, and power via engineering practice.* Rotterdam, The Netherlands: Sense Publishers.

Torres, V., & Hernandez, E. (2009–2010). Influence of identified advisor/mentor on urban Latino students' college experience. *Journal of College Student Retention, 11*, 141–160.

Torres-Ayala, A. T. (2009, May 18). Broadening participation in STEM: Not just an image problem. *The Hispanic Outlook.*

Torres Campos, C. M., Phinney, J. S., Perez-Brena, N., Kim, C., Orenalas, B., Nemanim, L., Padilla Kallemeyn, D. M., Mihecoby, A., & Ramirez, C. (2009). A mentor-based targeted intervention for high-risk Latino college freshmen. *Journal of Hispanic Higher Education, 8*, 158–178.

Trytten, D. A., Lowe, A. W., & Walden, S. E. (2012). "Asians are good at math. What an awful stereotype": The Model Minority Stereotype's impact on Asian American engineering students. *Journal of Engineering Education, 101*(3), 439–468.

Tsang, E. (Ed.). (2000). *Projects that matter: Concepts and models for service-learning in engineering.* Washington, DC: American Association of Higher Education.

Tsui, L. (1995). Boosting female ambition: How college diversity impacts graduate degree aspirations for women. *Annual Meeting of the Association for the Study of Higher Education*, Orlando, FL.

Turner, C. S. V., Gonzalez, J. C., & Wood, J. L. (2008). Faculty of color in academe: What 20 years of literature tells us. *Journal of Diversity in Higher Education, 3*, 139–168.

Turner, C. S. V., & Myers, S. L. Jr. (2000). *Faculty of color in academe: Bittersweet success.* Boston, MA: Allyn & Bacon.

U.S. Census Bureau. (2007). *The American community—Hispanics: 2004.* American Community Survey (ACS) Reports. Retrieved February 25, 2012, from www.census.gov/prod/2007pubs/acs-03.pdf

U.S. Census Bureau. (2010, July 15). *Facts for features: Hispanic Heritage Month 2010: Sept. 15—Oct. 15.* Retrieved February 25, 2012, from www.census.gov/newsroom/releases/archives/facts_for_features_special_editions/cb10-ff17.html

U.S. Census Bureau. (2012a). *Hispanic population of the United States.* Retrieved February 25, 2012, from www.census.gov/population/www/socdemo/hispanic/about.html

U.S. Census Bureau. (2012b). Table 229. Educational attainment by race Hispanic origin: 1970 to 2010. *Statistical abstract of the United States: 2012.* Retrieved February 25, 2012, from www.census.gov/compendia/statab/2012/tables/12s0230.pdf

U.S. Census Bureau. (2012c). Table 230. Educational attainment by race, Hispanic origin, and sex: 1970 to 2010. *Statistical abstract of the United States: 2012.* Retrieved February 25, 2012, from www.census.gov/compendia/statab/2012/tables/12s0230.pdf

U.S. Census Bureau, Ethnicity and Ancestry Branch, Population Division. (2006). Slide 6, *Hispanics in the United States 2006.* Retrieved February 22, 2012, from www.census.gov/population/www/socdemo/hispanic/hispanic_pop_presentation.html

U.S. Department of Education. (2007). The Integrated postsecondary education data system (IPEDS) glossary. Retrieved September 6, 2012, from www.nces.ed.gov/ipeds/glossary/

U.S. Navy. (2010). Navy reserve officer training corps—scholarship selection criteria. Retrieved July 19, 2010 from www.nrotc.navy.mil/scholarship_criteria.aspx

Valenzuela, A. (1999). *Subtractive schooling: U.S.-Mexican youth and the politics of caring.* Ithaca, NY: State University of New York Press.

Valenzuela, Y. (2006). *Mifuerza/my strength: The academic and personal experiences of Chicana/Latina transfer students in math and science* (Unpublished doctoral dissertation). University of California, Irvine, and University of California, Los Angeles.

Varma, R. (2002). Women in information technology: A case study of undergraduate students in a minority-serving institution. *Bulletin of Science, Technology, and Society, 22*(4), 274–282.

Varma, R., Prasad, A., & Kapur, D. (2006). Confronting the "socialization" barrier: Cross-ethnic differences in undergraduate women's preference for IT education. In J. M. Cohoon & W. Aspray (Eds.), *Women and information technology: Research on underrepresentation* (pp. 301–322). Cambridge, MA: MIT Press.

Vila, P. (2000). *Crossing borders: Social categories, metaphors, and narrative identities on the U.S.-Mexico frontier.* Austin, TX: University of Texas Press.

Vila, P. (2003). (Ed.). *Ethnography at the border.* Minneapolis, MN: University of Minnesota Press.

Visser, M., & Meléndez, E. (2011). Puerto Ricans in the U.S. low-wage labor market: Introduction to the issues, trends, and policies. *Centro Journal, 23*(2), 4–19.

Walcott, R. (2005). Outside in black studies. In E. P. Johnson, & M. G. Henderson (Eds.), *Black queer studies*. Durham, NC: Duke University Press.

Walsh, C. E. (1998). "Staging encounters": The educational decline of U.S. Puerto Ricans in [post]-colonial perspective. *Harvard Educational Review, 68*(2), 218–243.

Wasburn, M. H. (2008). One mentor or two: An instrumental case study of strategic collaboration and peer mentoring. *Journal of the First Year Experience and Students in Transition, 20*(2), 91–110.

Watford, B. (2011, Summer). This time, let's make progress: ASEE has a new chance to promote diversity. *Prism.* Retrieved February 29, 2012, from www.prism-magazine.org/summer11/last_word.cfm

Wieners, B. (2011, December 14). Lego is for girls. *Business Week.* Retrieved February 18, 2012, from www.businessweek.com/magazine/lego-is-for-girls-12142011.html?chan=rss_topStories_ssi_5

Winner, L. (1980). Do artifacts have politics? *Daedalus, 109,* 121–136.

Wright State University (WSU). Model for engineering mathematics education. (n.d.). Retrieved September 6, 2012, from www.cecs.wright.edu/cecs/engmath/index.html

Yin, R. K. (2008). *Case study research: Design and methods* (4th ed.). Thousand Oaks, CA: Sage.

Yoder, B. L. (2011). Engineering by the numbers. *ASEE profiles of engineering and engineering technology colleges*, 2011 edition. Washington, DC: ASEE. Retrieved August 27, 2012, from www.asee.org/papers-and-publications/publications/college-profiles/2011-profile-engineering-statistics.pdf

Yosso, T., Smith, W., Ceja, M., & Solórzano, D. (2009). Critical race theory, racial microaggressions, and campus racial climate for Latina/o undergraduates. *Harvard Educational Review, 79*(4), 659–690.

Zengin-Arslan, B. (2002).Women in engineering education in Turkey: Understanding the gendered distribution. *International Journal of Engineering Education, 18*(4), 400–408.

Index

About the Authors

Michelle Madsen Camacho is professor and chair of the sociology department, University of San Diego. Her PhD is from the University of California–Irvine in the interdisciplinary fields of sociology and cultural anthropology. She is a former Fulbright fellow and her ethnographic research was funded by numerous external grants. In addition, she formerly held two postdoctoral fellowships at the University of California–San Diego at the Center for U.S.-Mexican Studies and in the Department of Ethnic Studies. She publishes using both quantitative and qualitative research methodologies and engages theories from interdisciplinary sources including cultural studies, critical race, and feminist theories. Her most recent research on STEM education and Latinos has appeared in *Latino Studies*, the *Journal of Hispanic Higher Education*, the *Journal of Engineering Education*, and the *Journal of Women and Minorities in Science and Engineering*. She and her colleagues received the William Elgin Wickenden Award for the best paper in the *Journal of Engineering Education* in 2011.

Susan M. Lord is professor and coordinator of electrical engineering, University of San Diego. She received a BS in electrical engineering and materials science and engineering from Cornell University and the MS and PhD in electrical engineering from Stanford University. From 1993 to 1997, Dr. Lord taught at Bucknell University. Author of over eighty publications, her teaching and research interests include engineering student persistence, optoelectronics, service-learning, feminist pedagogy, and lifelong learning. Her research has been supported by NSF grants from programs including CAREER, ILI, S-STEM, GSE, and EEC. Dr. Lord has worked at SPAWAR Systems Center, NASA Goddard Space Flight Center, AT&T, and General Motors. Dr. Lord's leadership positions in engineering education include serving as president of the IEEE Education Society for 2009–2010, associate editor of the *IEEE Transactions on Education*, general cochair of the 2006 *Frontiers in Education* (FIE) Conference, and on the national administrative board of the ASEE Education and Research Methods (ERM) Division. She and her colleagues received the William Elgin Wickenden Award for the best paper in the *Journal of Engineering Education* in 2011 and the best paper award for the IEEE *Transactions on Education* in 2011.